I'M RUNNING

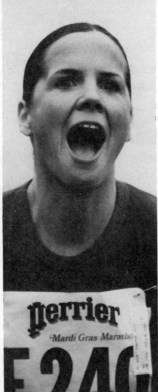

TO WIN

Tyndale
House
Publishers
Incorporated

Wheaton
Illinois

Library of Congress
Catalog Card Number
80-51698
ISBN 0-8423-1736-8,
cloth
Copyright © 1980
by Ann Kiemel.
All rights reserved.
First printing,
October 1980
Printed in the
United States of America

Pictures

page 11 ann with wayne,
documentary film
producer

page 29 ann with vladimir,
horst, and joseph in the
gymnasium

page 41 ann with pablo

page 81 ann with bev in
israeli marathon

page 96 rolfe and stephen
with ann and cindy

page 107 ann receives
minor first aid at the finish
of israeli marathon

page 128 ann talks to "her
kids" at the garden tomb in
israel

page 143 ann and tracy
after israeli marathon

page 148 ann and charlie

page 159 ann and jan

i dedicate this book to dreamers:

beverly wenshau, wife and mother and runner

jock semple, my trainer

cindy smith, runner and head of women's ministries
     for Fellowship of Christian Athletes, International

cleda anderson, a friend who believes deeply in
     saying *"yes"*

steve blum, road manager and friend, who clocked
     many of my miles

to *jinny muir,* my editor.
i really love you.

in a race, everyone runs but only one person
gets first prize. so run your race to win.
to win the contest you must deny yourselves
many things that would keep you from
doing your best. an athlete goes to all
this trouble just to win a blue ribbon or
a silver cup,
but we do it for a heavenly reward that never
disappears. so i run straight to the goal with
purpose in every step. *1 corinthians 9:24-26*

introduction

every morning, i wake up with a prayer:
"Jesus, i am just ann. my city is so big.
make me creative. give me ideas for my corner of the
world."

shortly after the 1979 boston marathon, and
meeting bev wenshau, a young mother from
minneapolis and a five-time marathoner, i
woke up one morning and thought,
"i know, Jesus ... i could become a runner
and meet all the runners in my city ...
and sing them songs and touch them where they hurt.
be a friend. maybe, *someday,* i can run the
boston marathon.
(well, You and i, Jesus.)

i did realize at the start that i came from a totally
nonathletic family. that i had never been a runner.
that i was thirty-four years old.
inherent in that tiny seed dream was the definite
possibility of failure. of never making it into
any marathon, especially the olympics of marathons:
boston.
of suffering and being vulnerable before the world,
and probably misunderstood ... and falling short
of the goal.

that is the way it is with dreams.
with being faithful.
giving one's best every day.

it is not:
          "Jesus, i will be deeply committed to You if You'll
          heal my brother . . . or increase my salary . . . or give
          me that new house . . . or make me famous."
      it is, rather:
          "Jesus, i will follow You to the end.
          no guarantees asked.
          no special rewards except that You will be at the end
          of the road to meet me when i get there . . .
      and i will know that i have lived my life out
          in truth.
          whatever is along the road . . . during the race . . .
          'yes' to it. to anything You bring into my life."

      but before i can write this book about faithfulness,
          i must talk about failure. one really is a part of the
          other. faithfulness involves the potential to fail . . .
          to fall short . . . not to win. to go for broke . . . to give
          one's very best . . . and still "miss the mark."

      the last couple of years, i have been trying harder
          than ever in my life to be obedient and true.
      just when i think i *know*, once and for all,
          where i will *never* fail again, i do.
      even in the last couple of weeks, i have stumbled
          and fallen hard . . . and climbed back up with my
          heart aching and my banner trampled and soiled.

      "they" (a production company) have been doing a
          documentary on my life. for weeks, i have had an
          entourage of fifteen or sixteen people following
          me around . . . with microphones and cameras and

the Lord God, the Holy One of israel, says: . . .
in quietness and confidence is your strength.
isaiah 30:15

12   all kinds of equipment. israel. rome. boston.
        chicago, los angeles. hawaii (where i grew up).
it can be very tense and pressured . . . and exciting.
    you become a family. eat together.
        travel together.
share intimate conversations and interviews and
    activities. and spend hours "shooting."
the film crew begins to know you very well.
    you develop a camaraderie.

this film crew was special. all young israelis.
they are the best in israel, and they were hired
    just to cover my marathon there . . . and some things
    with the children i took with me. anyway . . .
    as i broke out
with little songs for them, and spontaneous prayers,
    and they watched the love the children and i shared,
they were deeply touched.
    some tears were shed when we all parted,
    and i returned to the united states.

not long after, omri, the production manager,
    called the director in los angeles and said,
    "the men have big, international projects
    coming up,
but we keep thinking of ann.
    we would like to finish her documentary . . .
    do it all for her.
we will take a cut in salary if you will just
    let us come and do this."

it was very moving. young israelis in the
    film field work very hard . . . are very skilled . . .

have been in several major wars. money is extremely
valuable. this crew took a cut of $200 a day apiece, to
come to the u.s. and finish the documentary.
(Jesus did give me an idea ... that i should give
  them a percentage of my profit for the duration
  of the film. i surprised them with contracts
  promising it to them. they were very excited.
  and Christ's own chosen ones, who do not know
  Him at all, or call Him "Savior" in any sense, are
  touching truth. and truth will spring up in radiant
  hope sometime in their tomorrows. you'll see.)

all this background is to tell you about the failure.
  about the moments when i needed to be reassured
  that i was loved.
about the morning i got up in front of the crew and,
  in streams of tears, told them *i hated*
  the day before ... when they were all busy getting
  film equipment
and nobody even called to see if i needed a ride ...
or wanted someone to eat with.
  i was stuck at the hotel.
about the looks of sadness in their eyes.
  you could see they had given their best ...
  and i was demanding more.
about several of them who looked wonderful ... and
  carried that warm quality in their eyes. we found
  ourselves wanting to be close to each other ...
  closer than camera and across the room.
at moments i forgot it was an out-of-the-ordinary
experience for just a few weeks, with men from a
faraway country.
  besides, the project was for the glory of God
and not to nurture intimate relationships.

14   as for my running, my ego keeps creeping in.
         some moments, i find myself talking big to other
         runners, trying to impress them.
    underneath, i feel so inferior. so below par.
    sometimes exaggerating. pompous.
      many times, on my runs, God has reminded me
    He is not at all pleased with that.

in my eating i have failed, too. people say,
     "ann, if you run ten miles a day, and one
     twenty-miler a week, you can eat anything."
well, at times i have.
     twenty cookies in thirty minutes.
     half a cake.
     almost a whole recipe of cinnamon rolls.
not always, but often when i am frustrated
     and anxious.
     i know Jesus wants balance in my life.
     fat is not the issue, but healthy diet,
and self-control, and sensitivity to all those
     around me who cannot eat so much and stay thin.

failure. i do not like it. i resist it.
     resent it. do not want any part of it.
in the race, however, when all the stops are out . . .
     when i am going full steam . . . trying my *best* . . .
i still find myself failing.
     being reminded who i am not . . . and who God is.
     being brought down, over and over,
     to a humble place.
away from pride and criticism and a self-righteous
     perspective.

now, i will tell you my story.
    of running. of losing all my toenails.
    of living with swollen, blistered feet for weeks.
    of screaming and kicking and shaking my fist—
but being true to the dream.
    of two marathons run.
    one, at least, to go.
of all that God has allowed me to experience so i
    could write this book and understand His subject
    better.

bobby knight, head basketball coach at indiana
    university, says,
    "everyone has a will to win...
    few have the will to prepare.
    it is the preparation that counts."

i have tried to prepare. i have kept a journal.
    (because it is my story, it is built around "i".)

the end of the race is still far ahead. miles to go...
    but i run
        straight to
            the goal.

 april 16

the day after easter... patriot's day...
the boston marathon.
    cold, damp, drizzling rain,

thousands of people on the streets,
      mist hanging over tops of buildings.

there's something about that twenty-six-mile marathon
that overpowers me. men and women who work out
a hundred-plus hours a week, running ten miles a day.
      in rain. in cold. in sickness. through discouragement.
      alone. determined.
people who discipline their bodies and, even more,
      their minds, to run when they think they
      can no longer run.
      to push beyond the last ounce of energy.
      to feel the legs moving even when the cramps set in
      ... when arms become numb and almost paralyzed.

i sat on the windowsill of the second floor of the
      tennis-racquet club across from
      the prudential building.
      rain spitting in my face ... cold air on my skin.
thousands of people below with balloons and banners
      ... cheering ... pushing and shoving ... trying to
      see through fifty-people-deep.
then he came ... the first runner: number one.
      then the first wheelchair man, propelling himself
      by hand every inch of the entire course.
      later, the first woman. the sky filled with screams
of amazement and shouts of celebration.
      two black men running side by side, one's body
contracting in cramps so badly that it didn't seem he
could finish ... but he was only two hundred yards
from the end ... his partner sticking with him,
grabbing his elbow now and then ... to help him across
the line.

more interested in his ailing partner than in
making a good time or having a significant place
in the seven thousand entries.

i watched those lean, sweaty, weary bodies push on . . .
determined to finish . . . determined not to quit.
my eyes filled with tears more than once . . .
something about victory. determination.
running the race. running to win. not giving up.
putting oneself into life with wholehearted effort.
one day . . . one moment. the culmination of a whole
year. of thousands of moments of running . . .
when nobody else would run . . .
when one didn't feel like it.
the whole thing filled the spaces of life with
incredible power and courage.

i climbed down from the windowsill.
put on my sweater.
walked through the crowded streets to the subway.
quiet. thinking.
i want to run the race of life like that. my best.
500 percent.
almost crippled by the exhilaration . . .
and exhaustion . . . and demand.
accomplished. up at the front. moving the crowd.

someday i'd like to run the boston marathon.

someday.

april 17

lunch today with bev wenshau.
    she came from minneapolis with her family to run
    the boston marathon yesterday.
she'd written ahead, hoping to meet me . . . had read all
    my books.
suddenly, over lunch, she said . . .
    "ann, you could run a marathon. you're lean . . .
    and disciplined. you could."

i looked at this young woman . . . just my age . . .
    a hero to me.
    and at that moment, today,
    in the parker house hotel, downtown boston,
    the dream was really born.
to be a runner . . . to go for broke . . . not to quit . . .
    God helping me.

i wonder what this really means?

    i wonder.

april 19

got out of bed at six a.m.
    pulled on shorts, sweater, running shoes.
    sang, felt the morning air.
    ran and ran and ran.
tried to gear my mind to God's power.

19   committed myself to running at least
            one solid hour.
            headed across and down the charles river.
            passed other joggers.
        felt my fingers turning red, my legs going pink from
            chilly morning air.
        wondered if everyone knew i was a novice.
            a beginner.
        wanted to look tough, but not even sure what
            "tough" means.

        suddenly a bicyclist went flying by and screamed,
            "ann kiemel?!"
        i looked back and he was turning around.
            maybe twenty years of age.

        "you are ann kiemel, aren't you?"

        "yeah," i answered. suddenly embarrassed.
        shy. skinny. nonathletic.

        "i've seen you on television."

        "really?"

        "yeah," he said. "i've seen you several times."

        "wow. what's your name?"

        "bill."

        "hi, bill."

his eyes were filling with tears. he just kept
looking at me and saying,

"wow, i met you. i've found you."

"bill, what do you do?"

"i'm a janitor."

he must have been riding a long way on his bike,
because he lives in somerville, and that's far away.

"bill, have a good day . . . and . . ."

i tapped him on the shoulder.
his eyes were wet and red.

"there's a little song . . .
'God loves you and i love you
and that's the way it should be . . .' "

he started singing it with me. on a busy street.
in the middle of boston. on an early morning.
and i turned away. somehow the air was purer and
fresher. the sun was shining on the tops of buildings.
God's love was shining on me.

i ran on with new momentum and strength, and i sang
to the world. in my heart, i knew God had sent me
to that boy, bill . . . and God had sent bill to me.
and i ran and ran and ran. i wasn't breathless.
finally i stopped only because i didn't want
to overdo.

i listened to my body.
it felt good. easy. in tune.

i'm going to keep running.
i'm going to run to the end.
God is with me.
i'm going to win, and it's going to be a
great race.

april 21

in my heart, i know this running has
a divine purpose ...
initiated by a creative God.
i feel this goal of the marathon is going to be
one of the greatest adventures in my life.
one of the almost overwhelming challenges
i have ever faced.
i am scared.
it is something deeper than my running
the marathon.
it is the almost violent, stern test of
who i really am.
my guts. my "i can do it" determination.

i am standing before thousands who are watching.
waiting.
for years, i have told them to "watch ...
you wait ... you'll see ..."

well, now they are watching ...
and they are watching in dead earnest.

i wish i were as concerned about God's watchful eye
as i am about the human observers in my life.

"o God, make me faithful."

april 22

up at five a.m. ran eight miles in san francisco
   before my flight home.
   arrived in boston at 6:30 p.m.

i am lonely.

   several times i've started to pick up
   the phone and call any one of several men i know
   who would come
over as soon as possible. sophisticated, stimulating men,
who feel deeply about me.
   but i keep putting the receiver down, knowing
   these men do not stand for what i stand for . . .
   or believe in what i believe.
these men want more from me than i can give.
   to be obedient and true, i must stand alone for now.
   to be true to my dream, i must be pure.

well, it's nice to spill my feelings out on paper.
   to say simply and honestly, this is who i am.
   how i struggle.
   i am so human.

"Jesus, tonight i don't know what to do with me.
it's a warm spring evening. here i am . . .

    thrilled to be home.
    feeling sad and confused about loneliness.
even though in many people's eyes, i have everything,
    i really don't.
Jesus, thank You for the tests. for the tough places.
    for what You are wanting to teach me about spring . . .
    and warm evenings . . .
    and standing alone . . .
still and quiet . . . watching Your love develop
    in my life.
    thank You that when i am lonely, i am more
sensitive to the hurts and needs around me.
    alleluia. amen."

april 25

not long ago i got a new idea.

in the old ghetto building where children's
    haven is, there lies hidden
    a deep dark basement.
the plumber and i discovered it while we were
    looking for a place for the new bathroom.
(i had decided the people there needed more than
    one tiny bathroom with a rusty shower.)

    what if . . .
what if we could build a little gymnasium.
where children can laugh and play and grow.
where fathers and mothers can come too.
    where people might even find Jesus.

a couple of weeks later, i took an architect over
with his flashlight.
it was scary. i thought that any moment a rat
might run across our feet.

"sir, how much would a little gymnasium cost?"

it was a *lot*. a lot more than a bathroom.
gathering a group of committed Christian business-
men together . . . men who sponsor children's haven
in boston . . . i shared my dream with them.
they were astounded by the dollars.

"ann, we could never raise more than 10 percent."

"that is fine. i'll take care of the rest."

it was another dream. planted in my heart . . .
from somewhere.
if Jesus put it there, He would make it live.
i've often prayed:

"Lord Jesus, keep my books selling . . .
everywhere.
i need more money for my 'corner of the world.' "

the next day, after delivering valentine candy
to all the children in my neighborhood,
i crawled into the back seat of an old boston cab.
i had one more delivery, and it was too cold to walk.

"sir, could you take me to . . ."

"ann! hi . . ."

i know a lot of cabbies in boston. i sing them
    little songs every week.
we chatted. he asked me if i had any new dreams.

"yeah! you know that old building in the north
end, where i work with children? i have a dream
of putting a little gymnasium in the basement.
children could play there and find God's love there."

"wow. how will you pay for it?"

"i don't know. if it is God's dream, He will show me."

"ann . . . i don't believe in Jesus like you . . .
but i wish my kids had a place to play.
i'll help you. . . ."

my heart was pounding. stirred.
he pulled up to the curb to let me out.
pulling out a wadded-up old checkbook, he wrote
    me a check for $10.
it seemed like $10,000 to me.

that boston cabbie, in his beat-up old car, was the first
    one who really helped me with my dream. it
    became his dream too.

i shook his hand. i sang him a song and watched
    tears moisten his eyes.
he pulled away into the traffic . . .
and i stood on a street corner in my busy world.
sunshine . . . biting cold . . . horns honking . . .

thousands pacing their lives through crowded,
     narrow streets.

ann and one cabbie and Jesus . . . embarked upon a
     little mission that would some day stretch across
     the world. only . . . that day we did not know.

the architect was vladimir. the builder, horst.
     you would like them . . . my new friends.
every week i sang them little songs and surprised
     them with quiet prayers.
i was not very familiar with architects and builders,
     but they were people . . .
i know about people . . . beating hearts . . .
     strong, creative minds.
every week, over floor plans in our laps
     and discussions of basketball hoops and
     wall colors . . .
i reminded them that Jesus cared. Jesus loved.
     Jesus was in this project . . . therefore
     it was very important.

sometimes, horst cried. he has wild, woolly hair
     and a ruddy complexion . . . gentle blue eyes.
I could tell he was crying because he felt God . . .
     down in the basement, in the dust of that
     ugly-looking building.
horst and vladimir design and build some of the
     finest structures in boston.
their reputations are known far and wide.
     this basement seemed filthy . . . impossible.
     but not for God.
     with His ingenuity and inspiration,

He does seem to take the most obscure, ugly,
        unlikely places ... and people ...
        and create beauty and power.

    i haven't ever asked people for money for my dreams.
        i've tried to leave out fancy things from my life ...
        work hard ...
        use my own money.
    this time, though, people began to hear the story of
        the little gymnasium ... they gave
        without prompting.
    children and grandfathers and businessmen and
        young mothers. college students and janitors.
        people with a lot.
        people with barely anything.
        they gave and gave.
    every week the builder would call and ask how much i
        had to give him ...
    and his men would proceed to do as much work as that
        amount of money would cover.

    i got scared sometimes.
        some weeks we didn't have any money.
    the building inspector came and saw the rest of the
        structure.
    he was appalled at the poor conditions upstairs,
        and closed the entire building.
    it was going to cost a lot to fix everything above.
        sacrifices had to be made.
    once in awhile, i'd walk home from
        the little gym site, slowly ... heavily.
        would i ever have enough money?
        would the costs ever stop escalating?

could the dream actually live?
        i doggedly believed.

if you come to see the gymnasium,
    it may seem very unexciting to you.
on a dark, narrow street...
    clothes strung across a line.
    dogs yelping.
but big, bold new doors are on the front...
    fresh paint in the halls.
down in the once forbidden cavern, lights burn
    brightly. children play.
ladies bake cookies in the little kitchen.
in corners, people kneel and pray.
    Jesus lives there.

the man we found to run the gym program grew up
    in the very same neighborhood.
    so did his young wife.
years ago, as preteens, they had the same vision.
for hours, they dragged heavy wheelbarrows
    up and down the steps... filled with dirt.
they even raised $100 (a *lot* for those poor children)
    to make a little gym.
the money, of course, wasn't nearly enough...
    and the project too big.
    but God knew.
    He saw 'way ahead.

faithfulness turns out like that. it pays.
    even years and years away.
God never forgets tiny seed places deep in
    human hearts where visions are born and rooted.
    not ever.

patience develops strength of character in us and helps us trust God more each time we use it until finally our hope and faith are strong and steady. *romans 5:4*

6:15 a.m. . . . my hair pulled back and braided.
    bandaids wrapped around my heels and toes.
i have never dreaded anything so much as this run.
only Jesus can help me to be true to this.
    i will make it to *any* marathon only because He
    put it in my heart and will help me.

on the road i've been getting up at 4:30 a.m.
    steve, my road manager, had been getting up too
and clocking me before our early flights.
    getting up in the dark, in strange cities, is disgusting.
    (steve thinks so, too.)
each day i think, "i don't know how i can do it."

an hour and a half later. have just come back
    from my run.
    heels are covered with blood. blisters are big
    and nasty looking.
    but i feel great.
    i did it.
the hardest thing is just getting up and out . . .
    and the first twenty minutes.
it's like everything else. the tough part of
    speaking somewhere is catching the plane
    and getting there.
    taking the first step. the courage to reach out.
i ran ten miles today. i ran and i sang and
    i watched the sun coming up over the buildings
    of my city.
whatever else happens today, Jesus and i
    have already accomplished something.

may 13

mother's day.

far away from home ... from my mom.

a three-and-a-half hour layover in indianapolis.
    for lunch i had a poached egg on dry toast
    in the coffee shop in the airport.
i'll bet everyone else had home-cooked roasts and
    apple pie ... with grandparents ... and laughter ...
    and a long sunday afternoon nap.
    everyone but me.

i carried my shoes in my hands all through
    the airport because my feet were so swollen and sore.
    everyone stared at me. i was tired.
you know, if you give life time ... just a few hours ...
    a good night's sleep ...
    it always looks better. the tide turns.
i'm glad for Jesus.

i can't wait for tomorrow.

may 14

i have run the country roads of evansville, indiana ...
    the dark, rough city streets of detroit ...
    the farthest corners of norfolk, virginia ...
    the steamy, hot hills of charlotte,
    north carolina.

32　　blisters keep popping up. fierce pain.
　　　discouragement, determination.
　　my big toe is bruised and swollen twice its size.
　　　it hurts for anything to touch it.
　　sometimes i think i'm going to become a hypochon-
　　　driac just trying to get into a marathon!

may 15

sometimes i am afraid of dreams...
　　and of the world.
that i won't be strong enough.
　　that it will be over my head...
　　or the burden will crush me.
God, where are You?

may 17

i mustn't talk so much about running.
　　people are bored.
　　it is overpowering. it is unbalanced.
i must remember to relate to where everyone else is...
　　and not always to where i am.
i must do my running as unto God and not unto men.
　　every day i am a little more insecure
　　about running.
　　others are so much better at this than i am.

every night i sit in the kitchen, soaking my feet
　　in hot water and epsom salts.

33 sighhh.
i must not give up. must not compromise.
    i am running to win.

may 18

my big toe is seriously infected . . . close to systemic
    poisoning. a big blood clot.
had to cancel my speeches in idaho and montana.
    can't run for a week. confined to bed.
    i'm disappointed. so are those far away.
Jesus reminds me . . . it's *His* race, not mine.
    done in His time. with lessons to be learned.

may 30

life is only as powerful as its moments.
    a great life is not the result of
    a lot of money . . .
    or smashing success, or prominence.
it is great only in terms of how many
    significant moments there have been.
most people forget about the moments and strive
    only for the big events.
    i hope i remember the moments.

my great moment today is not getting a trophy
    or a raise.
    it's the moment i arrive at home.

knowing that tonight i sleep in my own bed.
boston outside my window.

good evening, Lord ... boston ... ziggy and patti ...
joseph ... andie and mollie ... joel.
i'm coming home.
i'm coming home *today*.

june 3

ran in pittsburgh today. ten miles.
hot. humid.
twenty minutes to clean up before speaking in a
big tabernacle tonight.

i am committed to running ... i am headed toward
the marathon.
but every day i have a new thing wrong
with my body.
a troubled toe. a new blister. a new pain.
it's *tough*.

but today i am a different woman from a year ago.
disciplined to run ...
to be earnestly committed to my Bible reading ...
to obey God.
i feel centered.

today i took joseph to dinner.
    he came in on the subway—my small, wonderful
    ten-year-old friend.
he ordered swordfish. we ate salad.
we talked about heavy things . . .
    like, he is 70 percent positive he will
    flunk fifth grade.
and yesterday he copied the answers for his
    math homework while the teacher read them off
    in class.

"joseph, that's dishonest."

"shoot, ann, the principal and my mom would kill me
    otherwise . . . what choice do i have?"

he is so young and simple and honest and up-front.
    with a good, caring mom, trying to put
    her best into his life.

we bought a box of brownie mix. baked in my kitchen.
    ate ice cream and warm brownies
    and watched "the muppets."
we talked about doing better at school . . .
about his mother really loving and caring for him . . .
that sometimes we forget he is a boy and not a man.

in the kitchen i put the leftover brownies
    in a paper sack.
    i wrapped my arms around joseph . . . looked into his
    black eyes . . . prayed for him.

let the children come to Me, for the Kingdom of Heaven belongs to such as they. mark 10:14

(i promised him a ten-speed bike if he would work
    harder at school.)
  God was with us right there by the stove.
i put him in a cab and paid the driver to deliver him
    safely at home.
his world is tough, but it is part of what will
    make him a great man someday.

june 28

joseph passed. he will not have to repeat
    fifth grade.
    i celebrate.
    i thank You, Jesus, for loving little boys
    like joseph.
    for having extra doses of grace.
    for knowing when life is too complex for him.
    joseph sounded excited when he called me.
    he is God's. a rainbow across a gray sky.
    a gold star on a window pane.
    a dimple in the cheek.
    atta boy!
    alleluia, God.

june 31

today i failed.
    i raced to the airport to catch a noon flight
    to denver.

got there late. all first class seats were taken.
only coach seats left. and today i just didn't feel
like being crowded.
i made a comment... sharply... about "why should
i ever fly united?... they make me tired!"
i had tears in my eyes. a scowl on my face.
boarded the plane, unhappy and unable to
thank God.

now the flight is almost over.
it's been fine. i've read ... napped ... prayed.
oh, i'm so inflexible. find it so hard to
bend with change.
to roll with the punches.
i get it in my head that something must be
a certain way...
and i don't want it to be different.
Jesus, i embarrassed You.
i am disappointed in me.

july 10

ran my very first race today...
the first time in my life.
lynn, mass.... a ten-miler.
i was the only woman in the race without a
boyfriend or another girl to run with.
terrified ... body tight and tense.
when the gun went off, it seemed as if
the whole group of entrants flew by me.
through the entire race
i wondered if i was the last one.

i ran and ran. i hurt . . . ached . . . wanted to stop.
   i didn't think i would make it.
at the ninth mile i turned a corner and
   twisted my ankle.
   maybe broke a little bone.
i hobbled until someone picked me up. felt peace.
   though i did not finish the race, i entered it.
   i gave my absolute best.
jock, my trainer, is going to take care of it
   in the morning . . . whirlpool . . . heat . . .
   that man is a real gift.

august 5

i have not run for three and a half weeks.
   not only have i not run, i have stumbled around
   in great pain every day.
jock keeps working on my foot.
   i'll have to start back at two miles a day
   when it heals.
   sigh.
you build up momentum and long mileage, and then
   you are put right back at the bottom again.
this is the fourth time i have been set back
   by injuries.

anyway, i am happy tonight.
   Jesus takes my weak parts . . . the negative feelings . . .
   the problems . . .
   and turns them into good
   every time.

august 6

a friend called tonight. a long phone conversation.
   i feel hurt.
she said i am the most nonintellectual person
   she knows.
   a strong statement.
friendship takes a lot of commitment and hard work.
   relationships offer incredible challenge.

august 7

talked to sarah. she's great with child . . .
   by an illegal immigrant who is not her husband.
but sarah is someone i deeply love.
   she is human and she has failed.
   but she is a fine woman.
she knows how to work hard. how to bring out
   the best in her children.
how to hang tough when the whole world is
   against her.
how to reach out to God and say, "i failed . . .
   i was wrong.
   forgive me."

she can laugh and cook and clean house better than
   anyone i know.
   i love her.
   i believe God is with her.
though i do not believe this pregnancy was
   God's will, i know He can work it out for great
   good in her life.

dear friends, let us practice loving each other, for love comes from God . . . . *1 john 4:7*

august 10

i've been sitting in boston airport for three hours . . .
   bad storm . . . flight delayed.
wish i could go home, but i have a convention in
   raleigh, north carolina, tomorrow morning.
   i'm hungry and tired.
   i dread getting in at midnight.
   my ankle hurts.
tonight, i wonder if i will ever run again . . .
   if the ankle will ever heal.
   if my dream is too great.

when God puts a dream in your heart, you must keep
   your eyes on the dream . . .
or everything gets blurred, confused, defeating.
   tonight i pray for strength to keep my eyes
   on Jesus.
   He made me . . . He is in control . . .
   bad ankle, late schedule and all.

   trust and obey.
   that is it.

august 19

walked to the grocery store . . . briskly . . .
   smiled at people who passed.
   sang praise songs.
   paced the beating of my heart.

43   good to be home and cook in my own kitchen
        tonight . . . chicken, green beans, mushrooms . . .
        no sweets, no desserts, no bread.
        i want to lose five pounds.
    hebrews twelve says it:
        "let us strip off anything that slows us down
        or holds us back . . .
        let us run with patience the particular race
        that God has set before us."

    at least once a year i must stay in my own neighborhood
        for a whole week . . .
        cook in my own kitchen.
        walk the streets.
        hear the sounds of my own city.
        eat fresh vegetables.
        be alone . . . quiet . . . separate.

        my particular race.

august 20

it's five weeks, and my foot still is not completely healed.
what if i have to drop out of the race . . .
    even at the twentieth mile?
what about all the thousands of people i have told
    about running the marathon?
they're counting on it . . . on me. they're watching.
    i get frightened about failing.
    have to keep giving it back to God.

this is His plan, not mine. His mission.
   He is my Hope and Strength.
   i am His empty vessel.

i've decided ... if i can't run, i will walk.
   i will not wait any longer.
there is heavy mist over the city ... drizzling rain.
   i'll go for fourteen miles today.

   ("run and not be weary ...
   walk and not faint. ...")

it makes me think of my friend victor oliver.
he is a great racquetball player.
he does many things well ... but especially racquetball.
in the last year, he has entered three major
   tournaments. survived until the finals, and then
   lost the championship by one simple point.

when he comes home, his young sons ask,
   "daddy, did you win?"

he tells them he played very hard ...
   his best ... for three or four days.
he tells them he wanted very much to win ...
   that it hurts a lot to lose.
but that giving one's all-out best effort is really winning.

those boys need to see their father fail sometimes.
   to hurt. to experience pain.
that is real ... that is life ... that is a piece
   of the victory.

(but it does not make it easy to be
so vulnerable . . . it doesn't erase the ache.
it just tests one's tenacity and commitment.)

august 21

it was hard, walking fourteen miles . . .

i have to keep reevaluating my motive for running.
is it really to glorify God?
or is it to glorify me?
is it to show the world that i am strong . . .
good . . . disciplined . . . determined . . . healthy?
is it to show others how brave i am?
does it matter to me who gets the credit?
if i work just as hard as someone else,
and the other person does much better than i,
am i happy with that?
am i willing to give my very best and leave the total
package of results in the hands of God?

if i give my best . . . and don't worry about
the result . . .
then i know my motive is pure.
then God will be glorified.

raymond berry quotes a verse over and over:

"whatever your task, work at it heartily, as serving
the Lord, and not men . . . knowing that from the

46   Lord you will receive the inheritance of your
      reward."

august 22

running is like finding Jesus.
    you start out with so much enthusiasm . . .
    so excited and exhilarated.
    so much momentum.
    ready to become a great runner.
what you don't know then is that it doesn't happen
    overnight.
it takes hours of courage and pain and hard work.
    standing alone.
putting more into the effort than anyone else
    understands.

it is one thing to find Jesus and another to commit
    one's life to Him and follow Him day in and day out
without demanding any promises or guarantees.
    just following Him because you love Him.

it is hard to drag my body out
    morning after morning . . .
    especially on mornings like this
    when it is gray and cloudy outside
    and so cozy inside.
it is hard to be disciplined and keep my eyes on
    the mark instead of on how i feel.

    Jesus, i do this in Your strength.

it is after midnight.

tonight was a tough test. these are vacation days
    and i have been alone.
at 9:30 i was hungry and popped corn.
    (what i really wanted was ice cream.)

a clear, cool summer night.
    i would have loved to share it with a man.
two different men called me tonight . . .
    terrific men . . . handsome . . . wealthy.
    i feel close to them.
    it would have been hard to stay true.
through the power and strength of Jesus,
    i obeyed.

my obeying God hurts those who don't believe Him
    more than it hurts me.
they don't get their way. their plans are thwarted.
    but i am safe and steadfast and sure
    in the arms and will of God.

obedience is the greatest source of peace and security
    to the believer.

as i obey God with regard to the men who
    want what i cannot give,
    i feel a growing sense of wholeness
    at the center of me.
the wholeness comes from saying "no" to wrong
    and "yes" to God.

this is also true in business negotiations . . .
it would be true of parents who obey the mind of God
in their relationship to their children.

there is pain in obedience . . .
but it is never so great as
pain in disobedience.
there is no desire so great as
the desire to obey God in my life.

the all-encompassing love of Jesus is what
first wooed and won me . . .
and i follow with joy.

(i'm glad for tonight. for the test.
i'll try to keep the song echoing through the corridors
of the world.)

august 24

i'd never make it without jock.

jock semple is very famous in boston and among
world-class runners the world over.
scottish . . . from the old country.
in his seventies. strong brogue in his tongue.
he tried to pull out the first woman who ever
ran in the boston marathon.
he had deep feelings about running being
serious business. an art.
he wanted no foolishness.

49   he began giving me little hints.
        having me come early, before his hockey players,
        and putting me in the whirlpool.
    massaging my legs, treating them with the care a
        surgeon or concert pianist would give to fingers
        or hands.
    while he rubbed, i'd sing little songs.
        talk about Jesus.

        "ah, shoot, ann . . . i'm just an old heathen. . . ."

        "jock, you aren't. you aren't.
        i want to help you know Jesus. . . ."

    jock signed me up for little races. watched for my
        face at the finish lines.
    he is salty and tough . . . won't give anyone the time of
        day if he doesn't want to.
    he is from the old school. not one to pamper a body.

        "all ye do in running is just let one leg
        fall in front of the other . . .
        that's it . . ."

    even today, i try to let it be that easy, but it isn't.

        "why, some of these clowns doing marathons . . .
        ye might as weel forgit 'em . . .
        slow as molasses . . .
        i kin walk faster than they kin run . . . disgusting!"

    there would be no marathons for me without jock.
        he is a best friend. drops all the small

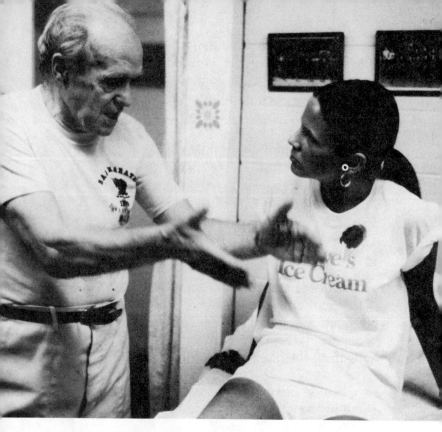

o Lord, Your discipline is good and leads to life and health. oh, heal me and make me live.
isaiah 38:16

and great hints that make one the best
long distance runner possible.

"ah, don't pray for me. . . ."

"oh, jock, i do . . . i do . . . always.
i love you, jock."

his office walls are lined with pictures of the greatest
   athletes of the twentieth century.
he is quoted in books and in newspapers.
   he himself has received several hundred trophies
   for running.
yet jock is one of the most humble men
   i will ever know.
he rides the train in on very cold mornings . . .
   is absolutely committed to making committed
   athletes great.

"ann, ye are making an honest man out of me . . ."

i really believe jock is making me a strong runner . . .
   and i am sowing in him the seeds of the kingdom.

this morning i was sobbing into the phone:
   "jock, i can hardly walk."

"what's the matter with ye?"

"i don't know. just got up to run my ten miles and
my foot . . . it's stiff."

still in my nightgown, i had hobbled across the room
   to the phone. injuries literally terrify me.

i have already had everything one can have and still
    be alive ... shin splint ... hamstring and
    quads pain ... achilles swelling ... groin ... back.

jock said, "put ice on the foot ...
    i'm going to get doctor mcgregor on the line.
    wait for my call."

(amazing people have come into my life because of my
    running!)

soon the phone rang. it was jock saying to get over
    to dr. rob roy mcgregor's right away.
    he would see me.
well, i knew of dr. mcgregor.
    the outstanding podiatrist in the u.s. ...
    had seen him on television.
it is very difficult to get an appointment with him.
    only jock could have arranged that.

hobbling into dr. mcgregor's office, i began to
    tell him about me.
    never had been a runner ...
    carried a dream ...
    was in training for a marathon in israel ...
    taking neighborhood children with me ...
    hoping to qualify for boston.
i began to cry again.
    "oh, dr. mcgregor, i have to go to israel.
    it's part of the dream.
    oh, doctor, are you a dreamer, too?
    i know Jesus will help you help me ...
    because Jesus is my song ...
    He's the one who's made all my dreams live."

he bandaged my foot.
      prescribed an anti-inflammatory.
      told me he would see me next week.
the way he looked at me . . . somehow i knew he felt the
      intensity of my heart . . . the pain . . .
      the fears surrounding "what if?"
      the sheer determination to do everything in my power
      to allow Jesus room for a living dream.

i took his hand. i sang him a song.
i walked out with my back straight, and my will
      shouting,
      "yes, we can, Jesus.
      we can."

seven days later, i sat in his office . . . much better.
      had used lots of ice . . . swallowed every pill . . .
      prayed . . . beseeched . . . interceded with God.
i had even flown to new york city and run the last
      eleven miles of a marathon with cindy smith.
      (people in the crowd that day had yelled, "hey, lady
      in the adidas, you look *great*!" i smiled and waved
      at them . . . they didn't know that everyone else had
      run fifteen miles more than i had! smile.)

      "ann," dr. mcgregor said, looking at me intently,
      "i want to help you with your dream.
      i'm not religious just like you
      and i don't carry dreams like yours . . .
      but i want to be a part of this one.
      it's a great dream. i've decided . . .
      i'll be your doctor . . . pay for your orthodics and
      shoes. you can call me from anywhere . . . anytime

. . . and i will take care of you. i'll help
                    God get you to israel."

and he did. to this day, i can hurry over
     to his office . . . without a scheduled appointment,
     and be ushered right in.
or call him long distance at any hour.
     he cares for my feet with gentle,
     loving conviction
     that they are called to carry messages
     to the world.
i pray for him. i try to plant little seeds of God's
     peace in his heart.

apart from running, jock and dr. m. and i
     would never have had anything in common.
today they can tell you about my many black and blue
     places and ugly, swollen areas . . .
     and tears shed without control after long runs.
they pace the dream with me through the valleys and
     up into the hills.
something happens when people share on that level.
     something deep and real and redemptive.

many other people have crossed my path
     only because i am a runner.
in cities across the united states, men . . .
     usually without deep Christian faith . . .
have run the country roads and city streets
     to help me get in my miles.
     they have paced me . . . encouraged me . . .
     given pieces of advice . . .
pulled quarters out of their shoes and bought me

cold pepsis when my face looked too flushed
and my body seemed to crouch too far forward.
and i have run ... and laughed ... and sung them all
    my little songs ... and talked about Jesus in
    totally unexpected moments ... spontaneously ...
    with enthusiasm in my voice and earnestness
    in my eyes.
many times, i would share my dream of the
    boston marathon and they would quietly remind me
    that there was always next year ... or the year
    after that.
i would run ... and shake my head fiercely ...
and tell them in no uncertain terms that I was
    going for
broke ... knowing that only Jesus could
    make it happen.
    that i would accept the year's results only after
    knowing that i had done my gut-level best.

a lot of men ... strong runners ... have smiled wryly
    and shaken their heads. some have said,
    "don't call us unless you do it ...
    we'll be waiting to see...."

running is the only thing that would have brought us
    together ... given us common ground.
    a place of mutual trust and respect.

today the world's perspective is so humanistic.
    "i can do it on my own ..."
    "i'll do it my way ..."
    "i don't need anyone ..."
as for me ... i could not have survived ...

carried the dream . . .
          without people.
          Christian people . . .
          unbelievers . . .
people who have checked my miles . . . and run all the
          distances . . .
and pulled my wet ponytailed head into their laps
          and let me cry it out.
who have fed me home cooking and bananas and
          bran muffins and cold drinks.
people who have marked their calendars and
          have prayed for me.
          family people.
          "acquaintances."
people behind big shiny desks . . .
          people in crowded neighborhoods . . .
people in ice cream parlors and hamburger stands.
          on padded pews in big churches . . .
          on park benches outside, where one only hears
the hymns through stained-glass windows.
they have all been part of the rivers in my soul.
          i love them.

people are important . . . they matter.
          i need you.
          you need me.
it is as important that i contribute to your life
          as it is that i let you add to mine.

the most beautiful part is that God provides me . . .
          you . . .
with people to help us accomplish His will
          in our lives.

He finds them and puts them across our paths
in the most unexpected needy moments.
He knows exactly what we need ...
and who can supply it.
people are part of God's end of the bargain
when we are faithful.

august 25

as i read God's Word, i realize that the men of faith
were the men who never gave up.
the tougher it got, the more they believed
and the stronger was their faith.

tonight i telephoned bev wenshau and told her
that the israeli government had invited me
to run the israel marathon ...
around the sea of galilee.
i suggested that maybe we could run it together.
her enthusiasm almost surpassed mine!

well, maybe i will run the marathon in israel,
but i don't think i'll ever make it to the boston
marathon. to qualify, my time for 26.2 miles has to
be under three hours, twenty minutes.
and my foot still is not back to normal ...
i've been walking my miles.
it's better than just sitting around and waiting
for my foot to heal.

sometimes in life, our spirits are nearly gone.
we cannot run.

we can barely drag our bodies around to take care
    of the details and pressures and demands of life.
sometimes we feel so crushed and broken and
    overwhelmed . . .
that we do not even see where we are going.
we are just out there walking to keep the
    heart beating . . .
    and the circulation moving.
but . . . if that is all we can do . . .
    and we are doing it . . .
that is still being faithful . . . not quitting . . .
    giving it our best.
    going on.
thank you, God, for that ability.

august 26

hartford, connecticut. really, danbury.
    a businessman picked us up.
i spoke to a large crowd in a stadium . . .
    outdoor bleachers.
    steaming hot . . . rain beginning to pour . . .
    drenched my hair . . .
    soaked my silk blouse and skirt.

"don't you want me to quit?"

"no . . . no . . . go on . . ." the crowd cheered.

so i gave my whole speech . . . everyone listened . . .
    no one moved.

a hundred and fifty people in that crowd
          came to Jesus.
          it was overwhelming.
      i was so tired ... finally pulled my wet hair back
          into a ponytail ...
          autographed that way.

          then it was time to run.
          ugh.

      one of the men took us to the hilly country roads of
          connecticut. it was hard! i was panting.
          four and a half miles.
          seemed like ten.
      we all cleaned up and went for a tasty dinner.

      i would have missed out on many things in life
          if i had not done them ...
          things i did not feel like doing at the time ...
          but disciplined myself to do ...
          and it turned out positive.
      just like the run today.

august 27

eggs and toast ... a rental car to branford, conn.
    a ten kilometer race.
    it was to start at 10:30 a.m.
david, my road man this week, went screeching into
    the parking lot at 10:20 ...
    all the runners were lining up.

i flew out of the car . . . signed my name on the
        dotted line . . .
        ran out to join the others.
    they had all been jogging around, warming up,
        stretching . . .
        and there i was.
        my second race.
    again, i was terrified . . . hot . . . and those *hills!*
    every time i turned a corner, there was another
        mean, nasty, ugly hill.
        my body screaming.
    began to walk up every hill as fast as i could . . .
        and run down the other side with forced speed.
    still came out number 6 woman out of
        twenty-five or thirty.

    i learned something more: hills are important.
        i must face them and work them . . .
        or i will never become a good runner.
    my heart has to be open to the hills of life, too . . .
        the tough places . . . the rough places . . .
        the narrow moments.
        they prove my worth . . . make me strong.

        our flight left at 12:05 p.m.
        david was waiting at the finish line.
    i jumped in and we raced to the airport . . .
        grabbed some water at the drinking fountain.
    boarded the plane (first time i've heard of
        pilgrim airlines) . . .
        in running shoes, sagging shorts, wet teeshirt.
        weak . . . tired . . . happy.
    happy that even though i might have done better . . .

61   and i was not a whiz...
       i did try... i entered... i finished.

   today, i am going to work harder...
       give more.

   in leviticus, God talks specifically about
       blessings for obedience.
   to obey is to receive His honor.

       "Jesus, on days when i would almost rather
       die than run...
       teach me to obey."

august 28

warm, humid morning.
   i don't feel like doing my morning run.
yet, for me there is no option.
to head for the marathon means
   i run when i feel like it
   and when i do not.
how i feel is absolutely not the issue.

now i am back from that run... i hated it.
   eight miles...
   feet hurt... breathing hard.
   thirsty.
   i pushed and pushed...
when i got back to my apartment, i stretched out
   on the carpet... and cried.

"Jesus, i cannot write a book on faithfulness.
i can't. i hate it . . .
it is so tough and scary.
it takes so much determination.
Jesus, help me to climb this mountain . . .
not to give up . . . to stay strong."

i reread this prayer by phillips brooks which i
learned from elisabeth elliot:

o Lord, by all Thy dealings with us,
whether of joy or pain, or light or darkness . . .
let us be brought to Thee.
let us value no treatment of Thy grace
    simply because it makes us happy
or because it makes us sad . . .
because it gives us or denies us what we want.
but may all that Thou sendest us
    bring us to Thee.
that knowing Thy perfectness, we may be sure
    in every disappointment
that Thou art still loving us and in every darkness
    Thou art still enlightening us
and in every enforced idleness Thou art still using us;
yea, in every death that Thou art still
    giving us life,
as in His death Thou didst give life to Thy Son,
our Savior Jesus Christ. amen.

i got up at 5:30 this morning.
    ran to the parker house at 5:45 and met david.
    we did four more miles around the common.
david said he was impressed with how well i did.
i sat and ate a slice of cantaloupe and drank a lot
    of tea and water with david.
then i bade him good-bye and ran seven and a half
    more miles.
    my step was light.
    the breeze was in my face.
there were moments when i felt tired ... but
    there wasn't a single moment this morning when
    i wanted to quit.

i sang. i sang, "it is no secret what God can do."
i sang, "i feel like traveling on."
i sang, "Jesus is the sweetest name i know."
    and my body felt light and moved easily
    i even passed other runners on the path ...
    felt alive and strong.
i had tears in my eyes as i cooled off this morning
    and sang, "there is praise and thanksgiving
    in my heart ... my heart is full of praise ...
    i will sing a song with thanksgiving in my heart."
    i sang it over and over.

i've realized today that He does pour water
    on dry ground,
    and He does put a song in a quiet, empty place
    and He does come when i can absolutely not go on.
He meets my need, and if i am faithful,

let us run with patience the particular race that God has set before us. hebrews 12:1

He proved to me again today,
He is faithful too.
if i step out and follow Him . . .
He will meet me.
He will match my steps.
He will order my days.
He really will give me strength for my day.
all i have to do is give my best and trust Him.

"i thank You for the river in my life today . . .
for the fresh, easy place."

i know the tomorrows are going to be tough.
i know september is going to be an incredibly hard
month.
i know there will be days when i drag my body out
and run
and it hurts . . .
and my hair is wet . . .
and i look terrible.
but i leave those days to Him.

i'm just thankful for today.

september 1

i like faithfulness.
i like being disciplined in running
because it helps me to be disciplined
in the other areas of my life.

i really believe that if we discipline ourselves
        in one area, it spills over
        and affects all the other areas.
    the more i'm disciplined in my running
        the more i'm disciplined in my eating ...
        in my Bible study ...
        in my exercise habits ...
        in my love for others.
    it all falls together.
    the more i look to God for obedience
        to follow Him ...
        not my physical desires ...
        or my ego needs ...
    the more He is the fulfillment.

    last night someone asked me again about loneliness
        and what i do with it.
    i think there is only one answer to loneliness:
        give your life away ...
        be a servant.

        it's true ...
        if we lose our lives, we find them.
        if we serve, we live.
    people go to parties ... drink ... beat their brains out
        in an office ... try to look beautiful ...
        just trying not to be lonely.
    what they don't know is that if they give
        their lives away
        and spend their energy touching other people ...
        meeting needs ...
        healing hurts ...

they are sustained and comforted and filled
with excitement and adventure ...
and the loneliness dissipates ... is gone ... lost.

today, Jesus, make me a servant.

september 2

cleveland, ohio, with tom and jan, my twin sister.
tom ran with me this morning ...
steaming heat ...
ten miles.
sore achilles tendon in left leg ...
but felt great in my run.

september 6

sioux falls, south dakota.
up at five o'clock ...
did twenty pushups ...
twenty-five situps ...
leg stretches.
it's still dark outdoors.
a runner is picking me up at 5:30 to do a
five miler before a 7:15 flight.

winning is being faithful
and faithfulness is getting out and doing it.
simply doing it.

i don't feel well . . . i'm tired . . .
   but that's part of it.
   part of the test.
that's what divides the strong from the weak . . .
   the halfhearted from the wholehearted.

back in 1899 theodore roosevelt said in a speech:

> *far better it is to dare mighty things,*
> *to win glorious triumphs,*
> *even though checkered by failure,*
> *than to take rank with those poor spirits*
> *who neither enjoy much nor suffer much,*
> *because they live in the gray twilight*
> *that knows not victory nor defeat.*

some people run scared, too intimidated to dare.
   to step out. to test new waters.
in being faithful to the "high calling,"
   there are moments when Jesus says,

> *"you may fail . . . but i dare you to trust Me . . .*
> *to reach for something great and good. . . ."*

i want to dare mighty things . . .
   stand on my tiptoes and reach.

september 7

aboard hughes airwest, san francisco.
   headed for pasco, washington.

69   some days there's a cloud.
            not often . . . just occasionally.
        it hangs low and engulfs me.
            i've been doing my miles every day,
            but i've got another injury.
        the achilles tendon is so painful i can hardly walk.
        i don't know how long it will take to heal.
            i do so want to run . . .
            to be normal . . .
        not always to be in the crisis of another injury.

        with daddy and mom yesterday.
            went to the beach . . .
            but i didn't have my good sunscreen with me . . .
            i got burned by the wind and sun and
                blowing sand.
        not enough to look bad, but enough to be harmful to
            my skin.

        well, anyway, here i go. in jeans and sweater.
            a couple thousand women are waiting for me
            this afternoon.
            i'll talk to them in pasco . . .
            i'll go in Jesus' name . . .
            knowing that when i am weak i am strong.

        yesterday i ate far too much . . .
            chocolate cake . . . pork chops . . .
            an artichoke . . . cookies . . . fritos.
        ugh. eating is so much fun . . . but i have convictions
            about staying in good shape . . .
            being careful . . .
            today i must watch.

70   people think i have everything.
they look at me and do not see any
    major catastrophes.
      they don't know i struggle with ordinary
      human problems that are built on ordinary
      human experiences . . .
      ego . . . insecurity . . .
      day in, day out frustrations . . .
as i realize how weak and human i am . . .
      how transient so many things in life really are . . .
i'm called back again to the quiet, faithful walk . . .
      Jesus with me . . .
and of knowing again that only He is eternal.
He brings the settling, centering peace on days when
    everything else is distracting and disjointed.

now i'm in pasco.

    i've checked into my hotel room . . .
    holiday inn . . .
about the three thousand, four hundred and
    ninety-first holiday inn of my life.
    but it's nice, clean.
the women are downstairs waiting for me to speak.

on the way from the airport i stopped at a
    doctor's office . . . he looked at the sore
    achilles tendon. he says it is a severe inflammation.
i'm to have complete rest. complete rest?
how do i do that when i have twenty-one speaking
    dates in september?

but this is God's plan and not mine . . .
    i must not get discouraged.

i must do my best and leave the rest to Him
   and trust Him.

   the women are waiting ...
i must get ready ... put on fresh blouse, skirt,
   and jacket.
   pull a brush through my hair.
even today i am glad God chooses me and uses me.

   He is good.

september 11

i'm on a twa flight from los angeles to san francisco.
   i'm discouraged.
in l.a. i did a free speaking engagement for
   the los angeles transformation center,
   a work with skid row men.
i decided what i needed after so many days
   on the road was to pamper myself.
went to beverly hills to get a facial
   and have my hair washed.
it cost a lot of dollars and it was all wrong.
   my hair was terrible.
the people tried to sell me new make-up products
   and became hostile when i wouldn't buy.
(i finally did let them talk me into buying a tiny bottle
   of wrinkle cream.)

   "every woman gets one of these ...
   it's a must ..."

when i examined my bill i realized that tiny bottle
    had cost thirty-five dollars.
    i was enraged.
    furious.
    (mostly at myself. and being thirty-four and
suddenly looking at diet books and wrinkle cream.
    boy, i didn't think this would happen in
    my thirties. . . .)
this morning i put on some of the cream.
    i can't tell the difference . . .
    but who knows?

september 15

washington, iowa.

    we flew into iowa city . . . rented a car.
before we got to washington, steve let me out
    and i ran five miles along the country road
    while he clocked me.
trucks zoomed by, pigs grunted as i passed their fields.
    i wobbled along through the gravel.
steve was angry when i finally got into the car.
he says i never pay any attention to the vehicles
    on the road. i just run as if i'm all alone in the world.
    he's scared i'll get "bumped off" somewhere along
    the way!

had never heard of washington, iowa.
    i'm amazed that people here even know who i am
    or have read my books.

warmed and touched that they should want me.
    happy to be a servant.

(i really did almost get bumped on the road today.
    i know that Jesus protected me.
He loves me and He's not finished with me.
    i also know i've got to be more careful.
i can't get my eyes so set on the goal that i forget
    to keep my common sense and equilibrium . . .
    and be in touch with the world around me.)
i thank God for safety. for reminding me that
    only following Him is what counts.
the end result is in His hands.

september 24

tyler, texas.

had steve drop me off six miles outside city limits.
    ran in 92 degree heat, 99 percent humidity.
(three flights today . . . sixteenth day on the road.)
    steve honks at the end of each mile.
i think he hates my running . . .
    my squeezing it into our already
    stuffed schedule.

    by the time the run was over i was soaking wet.
    unbearable heat.
the trucks along the highway would screech their horns
    at me. their air stream would nearly pick me up
    and blow me away. the exhaust fumes smothered me.

i had just twenty-five minutes to be ready to speak
in a city auditorium.

rushed in, just a few minutes late . . . and found
there was a musical presentation in progress.
it was two hours before that ended.
finally i spoke to the mass of people who had been
packed into a small auditorium for a long, hot
evening.
i tried to make the evening worthwhile for them,
putting as much as i could into thirty minutes.

as we drove from the auditorium to the motel,
steve began to reprimand me for being so much
into running that it was taking over my life . . .
there was something about my missing a dinner
engagement with a family . . . about their being
deeply hurt.
he was yelling . . . not at all like steve.

"steve, stop it . . ."

"i won't. i'm sick and tired of your running.
it's beginning to affect your commitment to
people . . ."

"steve, shut up! i can't handle any more today . . ."

(we weren't alone. i was sitting between steve and a
dear, godly woman who had come to see me.
a grandmother . . . saint . . . great friend.
i'm sure she was horrified by my
nonangelic performance.)
i was utterly exhausted . . . hurt, . . lost in the midst

of it all . . .
i just had to go on being "real."
in other words, screaming.

"i won't shut up. i'm tired of you . . .
of this determination."

"stop, steve, or i'll hit you," i said,
tears beginning to slide down my face.

"go right ahead."

he is 6' 2" . . . 215 pounds.
    he would never even feel it.
but it was the meanest thing i could think of.
    smile.

"steve, i fire you. . . ."

"good, ann, because i quit."

by now we were at the motel . . . i was sobbing.
    my shoulders sagged. dreams didn't pay.
they just got you into trouble. no one understood.
    i went to my room and started changing
    into shorts . . . teeshirt . . . running shoes.
dot, my friend, said,

"darling, where are you going? it's 11 p.m."

"i'm going to those people's house. i can't stand for
them to be sad. to have hurt them.
i don't care what time it is."

steve walked in.

"ann, you aren't going anywhere."

"yes, i am . . . and i am the boss."

"then i'll take you . . ."

"no! i don't want to be with you.
i don't understand you.
call me a cab. . . ."

"ann . . . please. . . ."

"no, i'm going. . . ."

i ran out, through the lobby, and into the back seat
of the waiting cab, clutching the address of
the people in my hand.

the cabbie said,

"lady, are you a nun?"

"a *nun*?"

"yeah, i think i saw your picture in the paper . . .
it said something like that . . ."

"no, sir. i'm a very ordinary young woman with many
flaws. sir, would you like to hear a little song?"

i sang to him. i could not bear for the day to be
wasted. for one more failure. i hated unhappiness.

he drove across town. dropped me off in front
        of a rather large, very dark house.
        it was now after midnight.
no matter how hard i knocked, no one answered.
only the dog barked and barked.
i sat down on the porch, buried my face in my lap . . .
        shivering . . . and began to cry again.

        "oh, Jesus, life is too hard.
        i just don't understand.
        i know i'm wrong . . . but i'm so confused.
        is it all my fault?"

suddenly the door opened behind me.
        i jumped up.

        "ann, what are you doing here?"

i flew through the open door . . . fell into their arms . . .

        "i'm sorry. i'm so sorry.
        i didn't know you were expecting me for dinner
        tonight. i did not know."

they fixed me hot tea, and said they were fine,
        and tucked me into a clean, fresh bed
        for the night.
the next morning steve quietly picked me up.
        neither of us talked.
he drove me out six miles from the motel and
        dropped me off to run the rest of the way . . .
        before we flew on to atlanta.

it took me a long time to recover from that.
            but i did. and so did steve.
        sometimes having a road manager is like
        being married...
            sometimes you love each other...
            sometimes you nearly want to kill.
            (my father would say, "oh, honey,
            don't speak so strongly.")

        honest living is having critics.
            is learning to say, "i'm sorry."
        is sometimes feeling weak... not strong.

        faithfulness means one goes on.
            gets up and pulls his or her shoes on
            and faces the next day and starts all over...
            trying to give one's best.

        faithfulness is "laying aside every weight,
            and the sin that doth so easily beset us...
            running the race with patience...."

        it is also discipline.
        i have realized through my running that a lot of
            people resent someone who has an ordered,
            organized live...
            resent your discipline to get out and run
            every day,
            or stay away from desserts if you are heavy,
            or get up an hour early to pray.

        today, people want life to be easy.
            free-flowing... undemanding...
            unstructured.

no one wants to be made to feel guilty
        because someone comes along and reveals
        guts and courage and stick-to-it-iveness.

one of my teeshirts says on the back:
    "no gain without pain."

sometimes i hate that teeshirt.
sometimes i wear it because it hurts so much,
and i have to keep reminding myself through
    every mile that the pain will someday bring reward.

not everyone needs to run ten miles a day...
or abstain totally from sweets. (i'd die.)
or meditate with God an hour and a half early in
    the morning.
everyone should feel the stretch, though.
    the pull of doing what is tough.
    what is not easy... but will refine
    and enhance life.

discipline says,

    "i am committed to something i believe is beautiful
    and good. i will pay a price for it. i will try not to let it
    take over my whole life, but i'll give it all i've got."

and the world stops and watches...
    because there is an essence... a quality...
    a magnetism that commands respect.

faithfulness makes ordinary people extraordinary...
    common people beautiful...

mediocre hearts brave ...
courageous ... unbreakable.

faithfulness takes a simple young shepherd boy ...
    lost in the fields somewhere,
    obscure ... unknown ...
and stands him before the unbeatable foe.
suddenly, all the years of tending sheep
    and killing bears and lions ...
    of using one's ingenuity in unknown,
    unsung moments ...
come to bear on this one hour in history ...
    when the world is watching.
    when life is at the crossroads.
one young david brings down one giant goliath ...
    and history is forever changed.

october 8

bonnie bell race. five thousand thirty women.
    my number was two thousand fifty-two.
    i was in the center of the crowd.
the first mile i practically jogged in place ...
    i could hardly move.
it took determination and strength and a lot
    of energy to push my way through the bodies ...
    in and out ... weaving between them.
i must have passed a thousand women.
ended up running about a seven-minute mile.
one of the first one thousand over the line.
    felt strong. my best race.
    felt humbled.

i strain to reach the end of the race and receive the prize for which God is calling us up to heaven because of what Christ Jesus did for us. philippians 3:14

i realize that if there were a thousand women
  ahead of me across the finish line, it says
  a lot about where i'm not...
about how much harder i have to work...
about how much farther i have to go...
  it was humbling.

sally and the children and joanne ferguson came.
  walked over with me.
clear day... winds gusting to twenty-five miles an hour.
afterwards, tom brown and his children, and virginia
  and carolyn and the whole group went for pizza
  and ice cream.
jerry dunfey called to say that he had seen me come
  across the finish.
  jock called to see how i had done.
  i felt tremendous love and support.
i felt all of that was affirmation
  of God's being with me.
i didn't want to forget that i was doing it for
  His glory and not for mine.
  my body felt strong.

no one can really understand what it costs or means
  to be faithful...
unless he has tried to do that.
the people on the periphery, cheering the winners,
  really have no comprehension of what it meant
to be out there running those miles.
they thought it looked great, and they were impressed
  with people who could...
but they couldn't know inside what it feels
  like to put yourself on the line...
  to compete... to feel the pressure and the strain
  and the throb in your whole body.

i think it's the same as being true with Jesus.
      unless one has really tried to be faithful . . .
          really paid some price for faithfulness . . .
      one doesn't understand the cost or the great reward . . .
          the pain and the great joy.

october 9

      did an eight-mile run this morning.
          stopped at jock's for a little bit of
          heat treatment on my ankles.
      patti lyons and her trainer, joe, were there too.

      as i proceeded on my run, Jesus showed me
          something . . .
      that i really started out to be a runner for
          His honor and glory.
      but i keep forgetting it's for His honor.
      i keep wanting it to be for mine.
      i keep wanting people to think i'm a good runner . . .
          to be impressed.
      i keep thinking they'll like me better and
          i'll be a better testimony to the runners
          if i am a better runner.
      but today, Jesus reminded me that i will never be
          any kind of runner unless He makes me one . . .
      and that all the commitment and determination in the
          world is not enough.
      and if i'm not genuine . . . if i am superficial . . .
          all the runners in the world will see through that.
          they will not be impressed.

84 they will not be touched by the heart of God.
Jesus reminded me again today that to be faithful
    is to be honest and real ...
and it's to remember that in the walk ...
    in the race of faithfulness ...
    He must increase and i must decrease.

the ego gets involved in faithfulness ...
    in wanting people to think we,
    in our own human strength and power,
    have done it.
wanting to forget that only He is strong.

i am so glad that Jesus forgives me ... this body
    of great human inadequacy.
i want to try to do better.

october 13

i don't know how to put all my feelings into words.
    the realization that in some divine,
    miraculous way God is with me.
that this is the greatest venture of faith i have
    ever embarked upon with Him.
that every day has got to be either a straight "yes"
    or an absolute "no" day.

i am in training for the israeli marathon.
    it is close to the time.
it is imperative that my body stay strong.
    that my legs hold up as i increase my mileage.
    that my endurance grows.

every day continues to be a shouting "yes."
    every day is a miracle.
every day i kneel and pray before i go out and run
    and when i come in.

i had flown into indianapolis after being in two
    other cities that day.
steve rented a car, and we drove to brownstown...
    an afternoon appearance to two thousand women
    on retreat. after speaking, i autographed books
    for women who were lined up clear through
    the hall and out the back door.
it was approaching evening, and time to leave.
we were to fly on to cincinnati for an appearance
    the next day.

    "steve, i have to do fifteen miles today."

    "ann, you can't! you have already been on several
    planes, and spoken and autographed for a couple of
    hours. besides, we have a plane to catch."

    "steve, i *have* to. i'm *committed*."

he nodded. by now he knows me too well to argue.
he handed me my bag and i trudged into the cold,
    gray restroom in this old auditorium.
    tears in my eyes. i hated running.
    but give up? i couldn't.
    not ever.

i pulled on my running clothes and started out.
    steve drove along behind me, with the sponsor,
    in the rental car... honking at the end of each mile

and following my ponytail and blue shoes
        wherever i wandered.
    he honked through fifteen miles.
        i never stopped nor slowed.
    i ran through dry corn fields . . .
        down long, silent country roads . . .
        over tough hills . . .
        through two more city limits.
    with dogs nipping at my heels . . . and steve
        gently nudging them away before they
        took real bites.
        33 degrees.
    i watched the sunshine . . . the sunset . . .
        then miles of darkness.
    i prayed that God would please keep skunks away . . .
        and kept trying to figure what i would do if
        one popped up and squirted me.

    when the run was over it was too late for our flight
        to cincinnati. so we drove.
    arrived and were eating our dinner at some poor cafe
        at 2:30 a.m.
        (what a good man steve is!)
    suddenly, we couldn't find the keys to the car
        so we couldn't get our bags out for the
        few hours left in that night. . . .
        our rooms weren't even very good.

    but nothing mattered . . . except one thing:
        it was a fifteen-mile day . . .
        and i had been true.
        and all the other pieces of the day had fallen
        into place, too.

steve had helped me.
Jesus had helped me.
everything was on schedule.

tomorrow will be a five-mile day . . . i'll be tired.
but whatever i accomplished today will not
be good enough for tomorrow.
it never is.
today is what counts.
in faithfulness, one never rests on past laurels.
not ever.

october 14

it was last night in brownstown, indiana,
that Jesus seemed to say,

"ann, if you go to israel for Christmas, to run the
marathon, take children with you. children from
your neighborhood. children who probably could
never go otherwise. let them walk where I walked . . .
feel the air on their faces . . . feel My Spirit in
the ancient walls . . . along the silent paths.
let Me touch them there so they can come home to
their houses and their blocks and neighborhoods . . .
and help you change boston."

i ran and i listened and Jesus was there.
i didn't tell anyone what He had said.
when i returned to boston, i called my accountant.

"ann, that is extravagant . . . it is a big project."

"i know, but i try to live simply so things like this
can happen. dick, it is Jesus' idea."

(my accountant says he never had a client
like me before.
he is learning to believe deeply in Jesus, too.
smile.
it's okay. he doesn't care if i tell you.)

i don't know what it is about israel.
i just somehow feel that Jesus is deeply involved
in putting this together.
it is His plan for me.
it seems so significant at this point in history . . .
the sea of galilee at Christmas . . .
jerusalem.
my heart cries out to be more at one with
my Creator . . .
more one with my Savior.
i read in psalms today . . .
what if God had not rescued us . . . what if?
we would have been covered over by the waters . . .
swept aside by the red sea.
but there are no "what ifs" in following Him.
He is faithful.
He is absolutely, irrevocably faithful.
day by day, His faithfulness is changing me.

october 15

shaker heights, ohio.

flew in this morning from cincinnati after just
   a few hours of restless sleep.
jan and tre met me. family . . . how beautiful.
   jan very pregnant.
   tre . . . strong and healthy and beautiful and bright.
   three years old now.
we had blueberry pancakes, shopped a while,
   then came home and all three piled into bed
   for a nap together.
i opened my eyes once to see this fine, beautiful boy
   between jan and me . . . asleep.
got up and pulled on my running clothes.
   dreaded starting out alone . . . but did a ten-miler.
   i did it in less than eight minutes to the mile.
   praising the Lord.
running through the shaker heights suburb to the
   ream house . . . thinking of how the Lord has
   blessed jan and me.
jan in her suburban home with a handsome,
   wonderful man
   and a beautiful child. jan, ready to bring
   another child into the world very soon.
and i, trying to follow Jesus in my own way . . .
   challenged and thankful.
"this is the day the Lord has made."
   i really rejoice.
it's another "yes" day toward israel.

propped up in bed. cool, overcast day. my heart is
    overcast, too.
i feel pain up the backs of my legs and don't feel
    that i should get out and do my miles today.
    afraid of an injury.
i realize again what a miracle this adventure is ...
    what an impossibility apart from the power ...
    and the grace ... and the spirit of Jesus.
He's the one who will make it live ..
    who will make it work ...
    who can keep my body strong.
today, again, i surrender ...
    the marathon ...
    the trip to israel ...
    whatever it means.
i long more—much more—for Him ...
    for His presence and power in my life.

faithfulness means facing issues over and over again.
    issues like integrity ... our honesty ...
    how we are coming across to the world ...
    facing ourselves ... our flaws ... our weaknesses.
it's painful to do that ...
    to be moving along feeling centered and
    at peace ...
    and right with God and the world ...
and suddenly to be stopped ...
    and to reevaluate and realize that maybe
    things need to be cleaned up and redone
    in our lives.

3:30 a.m. my brother fred called.
   they have a baby girl.
   flawless ... seven pounds, eleven ounces.
   tasha michelle.
   a miracle.
a brand new, small, tiny, sweet human being.
   blonde. a dimple in her chin.
   a healthy body. a healthy mother.
   a joyful dad.
   and i ... a blessed aunt.
   alleluia, God!
if we give Him time, He does everything beautifully.

8:30 p.m.
   ran thirteen miles today.
   had lunch with cindy smith from fellowship of
christian athletes. she is running the
   new york marathon.
   she was inspired, she said,
   when she heard me speak.
she's going alone, and i decided to go with her ...
   to fly in saturday night ...
   to eat spaghetti with her ...
   to meet her at the fifteenth mile with a cold drink
   and to run the last eleven miles with her.
i feel Jesus put it into my heart ...
   not to let her do it alone.
nobody can identify better than somebody who's been
   in training ... who knows what discipline and
   courage it takes to stand alone and dream that
   dream. we all need each other ... and not just
   runners.

as i ran today ... and worked in my office ... and
talked with little joseph on the phone ...
i thought of this important message about
faithfulness ...

it pays.

there are lots of faithful days when it doesn't seem
to be worth it ... and it hurts like everything ...
and nothing seems to count ... and add up.
but it pays.
i'm grateful for that tonight ... following Jesus ...
giving my best one day at a time.
it pays.

Jesus says there is evil in the world ... but He
says, "don't be overwhelmed by evil.
overcome evil with good."
that's my prayer as i think of taking children
to israel with me ...
of touching their lives ...
of knowing that all around them and even in them
there is human weakness and brokenness
and struggle and pain.
but if i can give them a glimpse of Jesus,
of His power,
maybe i can overcome the evil with good.

october 20

two months from today ...
the sea of galilee marathon ...

jerusalem.
my very first.
today i passed another big test...
had much pain in my foot this morning...
spent two hours at dr. mcgregor's being
reassured that it would be okay.
walked out with my foot taped up...tried to run
and couldn't so much as hobble half a block.
put ice bags on it...
spent the night at raymond and sally's...
said deep down within me,

"Jesus, what is it i need to learn?"

got up this morning...trusting.
went out with sally and did two miles.
exuberant...overwhelmed.
went out and did another five.
could have done more.

i keep thinking of gideon. anyone in his or her
right mind would have thought that
thirty thousand men would be a lot stronger than
three hundred.
but Jesus taught them...and He's teaching me...
that it's not by power or might,
but by His spirit and His wisdom alone.
the dream of the trip to israel...
and the children...
and raymond and sally and joanne
and all of us going seems to be blossoming
into something more beautiful and significant
every day.
we are all standing back to watch the hand and the

power and the mercy of the Lord.
we can make our own plans and put together our own
    things, but when Jesus puts together our package,
    it has a dimension and a breadth that no human
    plan could possibly contain.
His ways are best.

raymond and i have talked a lot today about balance.
    balance in our lives . . .
    on a football field . . .
    in my training to run . . .
    in the way we follow Jesus . . .
    our theology.
how biblical it is. what an important part of
    faithfulness balance is.

on this clear, fresh, balmy fall evening . . .
    with leaves glowing in warm oranges and yellows . . .
    there's wild celebration . . .
    my heart is quiet . . . but alive . . .
    beating strong with the love and the hope of
        Jesus.
    He is everything.
    He is all there is.
and if He is lifted up, all men will be drawn to Him.
    alleluia.

october 21

i'm back from new york city . . . from running with
    cindy in the marathon.
last night, after fettucini and spaghetti at

mama leone's with cindy and linda and carol
and little john, i asked cindy,

"how did we ever get into this dream of
running marathons?"

i was probably more scared for her than she was . . .
and scared for myself because i had promised
to run the last eleven miles with her.
still worried about my foot.
got up at five this morning . . . did warm-up exercises
with cindy . . . had a piece of toast with her . . .
hugged her goodbye as she went out the door.
met her at the fifteen-mile mark . . . ran the eleven
and a half miles to the finish.
the crowds were cheering.
cindy never flickered . . . reached out to people . . .
talked to them . . . responded to them.
i learned a lot from her . . . to relax . . .
to enjoy the crowd.
to experience the race for the right reasons.
it was a day i will never forget. running with cindy.
knowing that soon, the Lord willing, i will be doing
my own marathon.
feeling my body strong and my foot good after all the
injury and the fear.
realizing when it was all said and done
that a marathon in and of itself
is an empty goal . . .
that anything in life is empty . . . except as it is
linked to Jesus . . . to His purposes and plans.
i relinquished my dream of the
israeli marathon today . . .

they that wait upon the Lord shall renew their strength. they shall mount up with wings like eagles; they shall run and not be weary; they shall walk and not faint. isaiah 40:31

of taking the children . . . of all that it seems
   to hold that is beautiful and good.
   and somehow, as i relinquished it,
   i felt God giving it back to me.
i felt a confidence that my body would stay strong . . .
   that He's really going to help me these
   next two months.
   i'm so glad for Jesus.

october 23

i spoke last night in a large catholic church.
   the response was beautiful.
a girl who had been one of my students at
   eastern nazarene sort of came out with the fact that
   she likes women better than men . . .
   doesn't believe in Jesus Christ . . .
   believes in reincarnation . . .
and that we're all just a part of some energy process.

i walk away feeling empty and troubled when i hear
   someone talk like that.
i really care about this girl and know that
   she's been through a struggle and a darkness that
   only God can really understand.
i know i need wisdom . . . and i pray for truth.

sometimes i am so busy and pressured . . . i forget to
   remind the people closest to me that
   i really love them.
called andie this evening to check on things
   in the office.

98   said to her ... "i really love you,
          do you know?"
          and andie hesitated and said, "do you?"
    i realized again how much i fail at times to let andie
          and others around me know how significant they are.

    i think of a thousand things i need to cover ...
          people to call ... to talk to ...
          to check with ... to see.
    every day it seems i can never do enough to fit
          everything in.
    i guess my responsibility is to be faithful ...
          to give my best today and know that tomorrow
          God will help me go on from there.
    and on that level ... somehow ... Jesus and i together
          won't fail.

    psalm 138, the last verse ... "Lord, your love is eternal.
          complete the work that you have begun."
    this morning that is my prayer.
    i don't know where it will lead me or what it will
          mean ... but i want Him to complete the work
          that He has begun in my life ...
    that will bring honor and glory to Him ... amen.

november 1

    portland, oregon. i woke up in my little motel room ...
          and i couldn't even remember where i was.
    next i felt pain in my foot and thought of the
          ten miles i must run today ...
    where would i run those miles in portland?

every day . . . a new city . . . a new place to run.
      a new stretch of faith.

      i've been thinking about how faithful Jesus is.
      He must be shaking His head at me and saying,

            "ann, you're like the children of israel.
            i give you jock.
            i give you dr. mcgregor.
            i give you some great runs in between
               the bad ones
            just to remind you that i'm there.
            i give you people who love you and are
            praying for you . . .
            an exciting mission . . .
      and you still doubt and fear and get discouraged."

      last night i spoke at a college here in oregon.
         afterwards i sat at the autograph table
         while several hundred people swarmed past,
         trying to get close for my signature.

      just as i was starting to sign a book, a young man's
         face appeared through the crowd.

         "ann, i want to say something," he barked out.

      i stopped . . . looked up . . . felt a little uneasy.

         "yes?"

         "i heard you tonight. it was disgusting. you are a
         real phony. you use your neighborhood to make
         yourself look good. to build up your own ego."

i felt my face getting very hot. my forehead damp.
   not moving . . . hardly breathing . . . i just sat there
      watching him. listening.
   the crowd of onlookers was suddenly silent. listening.

   "ann . . . i just don't buy it. i'm disappointed."

   "what is your name?" i asked quietly.

   "marty."

   "marty, thank you for being honest. that takes a lot
   of courage. my first reaction is to say that it's not
   true . . . what you said. not true at all. but then,
   i know i am human, and have blind spots. only God
   really knows truth. pray for me . . . and don't worry.
   if what you say about me is correct, God will take
   care of it. He will bring purifying things into my life."

marty stared at me for a moment, then faded away
   into the crowd.
i went on signing books. some people tried to
   reassure me . . .

but i must listen when criticism and discouragement
   come along.
there is usually some thread of truth in any
   criticism.
when one really wants to be faithful, discouragement
   comes. sometimes gradually, over a long
   period of time.
   sometimes suddenly . . . acutely . . . stabbing.
discouragement is not bad. not negative . . .
   unless we let it overpower us . . .

warp and cripple us.
sour us . . . make us bitter.
discouragement can bring us back to the center . . .
slow us down . . .
remind us that we are weak.
only God is strong.
strength is really perfected in weakness.
we are forced to reevaluate . . . to reassess.

this was one of the heavy times.
i try to ride with it . . .
let it settle me the way it is supposed to.
i must not fight it or kick it away.
i just wear it . . . but lightly.
laugh in the midst of it. still wrap my arms around
the world . . .
smooth the crooked places in people's lives.
in time the hurt goes away and my eyes have a
warmer look.
my heart a more gentle rhythm.

november 3

this week i had the privilege of running with
jeff wells and john bodwick . . .
two world class runners preparing for the
olympics . . .
strong, believing young men with hearts for God . . .
who want to glorify Him.
we did a fast ten-mile run.
ate peanut butter cookies.

warmed up together . . . ate a bite of lunch.
i wore john's shorts and jeff's teeshirt.
i knew that Jesus had given me those runners . . .
   to encourage me
   at this particular low point in my
   preparation for the marathon.

today i keep feeling this treasure hidden
   in my heart.
i realize that however faithful i am,
   if i am not faithful for His sake,
   it's just trash.
this is the treasure . . . to love Jesus
   with all my heart.
   to represent Him truly, purely, genuinely
   in the world.

i've been reading about david and goliath.
all the people saw things from a human standpoint . . .
   david saw things that were not seen.
he went in the fear and grace and wisdom of the Lord.
   he was victor.
i face the marathon in the same perspective.
it seems impossible . . . i've not been running
   very long . . .
   it's still a long way.
   i have a low pain threshold.
   i'm scared . . . i'm tired.
but i go on in the might of the Lord . . .
   He has sent me . . . He will be with me.
   i have peace . . . real peace.
   amen.

november 5

boise, idaho. ran eighteen clocked miles yesterday . . .
  but because of the mountains, it seems like
  a lot more . . . up and down!
saw old college friends last night in nampa . . .
  after i spoke, a whole group of high school
  girls came up to the autographing table and
  said they wanted to run with me this morning.
pulled myself out and met six or eight of them
  at seven o'clock. also a couple of
  eleven-year-olds.
we did a fast five-mile run . . .
  had big glasses of cold water and orange juice
  in the coffee shop.
  good to have their support.

felt ill later in the day . . .
  i must keep my eyes on who God is
and not on the situations and responsibilities that
  get to be a burden.

november 6

  kansas city. flying today to lexington, kentucky,
  and cindy smith's home.
this is one of my weeks of intense training before
  israel.

even before sunrise, i could hear the wind howling.
  wind-chill was below zero.

"o God, i really hate this.
            i hate to run."

i did some Christmas shopping for my family today.
the wind ripped through me . . . i couldn't get warm.
my mind was clouded with dread at the thought of
      getting out again the next time to run in the
      cold wind . . . of pulling on running shoes *ever*
      again the rest of my life.
i dropped in at a winchell's. ordered one huge
      cinnamon roll.
      inhaled it and ordered another.
      my body and mind were begging for strength.
suddenly, i spotted a pay phone on the wall.
a man was sitting very close to the phone, but i
      edged over with my little phone book and
      began calling people long distance.

      "daddy? it's ann.
      oh, daddy, pray. it's dark.
      sometimes i think i'm going under."

(the man near the phone seemed to lean a bit closer.)

      "cleda, i'm calling from k.c.
      oh, cleda, this dream is so tough.
      some days i'm sure i can't make it."

      "sally, are you praying? . . .
      but i mean are you and raymond really praying *hard?*
      the world looks dark . . . i'm dying . . ."

i found myself crying. pouring out my heart to
      everyone who came to my mind to call.

then it was time to pick up and move on.
    beyond the tears and the fears.
    to go shopping for my family's Christmas.
as i walked out the door of winchell's
    i saw that man staring at me with a really
    frantic look.
he probably thought i was in the middle of a
    divorce or financial ruin...
    and i was walking out to commit suicide!

but that's not the end of the story.
today i went beyond what i had been capable of.
    i broke through the possibility barrier.
    i turned a corner.

cindy and i went out for our ten-mile run.
    about five miles into it, the thing i had dreaded
    finally happened.
    it was the worst...the bottom.
    i could hardly breathe...
    every muscle throbbed.
inside, i was screaming and yelling and shaking
    my fist at God.

    "how could You call me to this?
    i can't do it...i can't stand this pain any longer.
    i won't..."

suddenly i turned to cindy. wheezing, i choked out:

    "i'm not going to israel!"

    "kiemel!..."

"i mean it.
and i'm not ever doing a marathon . . .
anywhere . . .
i hate it . . . running . . . *hate* it."

by now the tears were streaming.

"ann, you've done hundreds of miles.
you can't let it go to waste . . .
don't throw them all away. . . ."

"cindy, i don't care."

she pulled me down on the grass.
i pulled off my shoe where the blister was smarting.
she tore off a bandaid from her ailing toe and
stuck it across my red, swollen foot.
she gave me her right shoe and took mine.
there were no words.
i crawled back up to my feet and started picking
up the rhythm of the hill.
her shoe on one foot . . .
mine on the other.
she came up from the back and we began to push the
remaining miles behind us.
even in the cold, sweat began to trickle down our necks.
no hill or passing car or strip of color in the sky
mattered. i was lost in a world of the most
intense concentration.
i thought if i could just get to the black mailbox
outside cindy's house,
i would make it.

when the way is rough, your patience has a
chance to grow....when your patience is in
full bloom, then you will be ready for anything, strong in character, full and complete.
james 1:3, 4

the stomach cramps ... chills ... the run ...
        it's all behind me.
        Jesus and i did it.
    i will never have to go back to where i was
        before this morning.
    the process has led me here by bits and pieces ...
        day by day.
    death to a vision before a vision can live.
    death to the ego and the human will
        that would corrupt and pollute that vision.

        death at last.
        the crisis past.
        the turning point in the road.

november 11

midnight ... defiance, ohio .... holiday inn.

did twenty-one miles yesterday.
though my foot is swollen, i felt strong and good.
    had another argument with steve tonight
    about my running.
he says it is coming before my speaking.
    is he right?
i know that i really need Jesus ... His direction ...
    His wisdom ...
    and i want His will.
my sharing His love with people *must* be a priority ...
    must be given my best.

that's another lesson about faithfulness...
        not only *how* to be faithful...
but to know which things should come first and
    receive my faithful efforts...
how to keep it all in balance.
    being faithful to God's will
    and not to ann's ego.
tonight it's impossible for me to discern.
    i beg for His guidance.

recently i needed a large sum of money for a
    very special project.
        my accountant said we were going to be short
        of the necessary funds.
i had gathered all my resources...even a miracle
    loan from the bank. i had nothing left.

i was not worried or upset, though.
it was something i had believed deeply about...
    all that mattered to me, anyway,
    was God's will.

it was the final hour. i took my accountant and
    another businessman up to my apartment to make
    the decision because my office was crowded with
    people, and this was a major, monumental moment.
it was shortly after noon...the middle of the week.

my accountant finished his remarks with...
    "ann, i think we will have to liquidate it...
    recover what we have put in...and..."

i interrupted with a quiet prayer.

110   they sat there, watching me.
       i proceeded, with my eyes open (that's how i
          always pray) . . .

         "Jesus, i love You.
         i love You today.
         i am not worried.
         what You want is what i want.
         some of the people downstairs,
         and maybe dick (my accountant)
         too, are more worried because they do not know
         You like i do. You have never failed me. i trust
         You now to 'make the way straight.' "

before any of us could open our mouths,
     the phone rang.
my unlisted phone in my apartment, where
     i almost *never* am in midday.
my first thought was that it was andie, my secretary.

        "hello."

        "ann, this is _____ .
        margaret and i were just out taking a walk in the
        country, and the Lord seemed to impress upon us
        to call you . . . that you needed something."

friends . . . thousands of miles away, from the midwest.
     land developers.
we had not talked in months.
     besides, i would never ask anyone, ever, for money.
     i am shy even talking about it.

when i could regain my composure, i told him it was a
miracle he called. that i did need something. could
he and margaret just pray?
the end of the story is that he borrowed the money
for me ... at low interest ... that i can pay back
through the end of the year.

we sat in my living room and cried.
    even my accountant.
it was the kind of thing i have heard people relate,
    but had never experienced personally.

it told me that the project was genuinely in God's will.
    it was a "yes."

people say, "ann, how do you *know* God's will?"

    how did i know the gymnasium was right?
    trying for the boston marathon?
    going to israel with twelve children?

dedicated followers of Jesus want God's will.
    i believe that.
we just do not always know what it is.
    how to read it.
    to make sure it is His idea and not ours.

i have often not known if it is God's plan
    or something i have cooked up.
but time always reveals that.

take the seed idea and give it room to grow.
    do not push it ... or shove it out in front ...
    or manipulate things around it.

allow breathing space.
stay yielded and open before God
    and do not develop strong attitudes either way.

either the plan or idea will take root or not.
doors around it will continually open . . . or close.
it will be followed by "yes's" or "no's."

what about my project that had the miracle loan?
    well, we are not far enough along, yet, to know if it
    is going to be a great blessing.
i do know that if the whole thing flops,
    i have followed only the "yes's."
there have never been any "no's" relating to it,
    up to this moment.

in major job moves in my life . . .
    in crisis decisions . . .
i have never had God write on the walls or speak in an
    audible voice.
i have prayed earnestly. have asked good friends'
    (and my parents') advice.
weighed the positives and negatives.
then i have made a decision . . . what i believed,
    from the data i had, to be best and right.
always, i have prayed . . .

    "Jesus, this seems to be the way.
    if i am wrong, please slam the door,
    loudly, in my face."

then i have moved forward, knowing that God,
    whom i serve and love, and who i believe is vitally

interested in me, will care enough to turn me around
        if i am wrong.

faithfulness is taking one day at a time.
    responding to every whisper and call.
    (knowing that some whispers are deceivers . . .
    so staying very close to the Leader.)
letting Him show me in ways He knows
    i will understand.

and in moments when we are totally confused . . .
    and lost in the fog . . .
we must be willing to stand still. do nothing . . .
    let the issue rest, believing that if He is given enough
    time, He will clear the path . . .
and spray the sky with sunlight and promise.

november 12

this morning steve drove me ten miles out on a
    country road . . . dropped me off . . .
    i ran all the way back to the holiday inn.
    ten-mile run . . . sixty minutes.
    my best time.
it was cold and i wanted to stop . . . but i
    kept on running.
trucks nearly blew me over . . . but i waved to
    each person . . . .
    i sang . . . i celebrated when it was done.
    it was a big "yes."
(this is the day after steve . . . and God . . . really
    prodded me hard about feeling sorry for myself . . .

114   for wanting to give up ... for wanting easy
           dreams ... for doubting God ...
           for forgetting to keep my confidence in Him.
           Jesus did something special for me yesterday.
           i was changed.)

november 14

youngstown, ohio. another beautiful day ...
    God's victory.
ran on the golf course ... met new people.
spoke to an over-capacity crowd in the
    methodist church.
Jesus lives ... His love changes me.

jan's baby is due any moment. we wait with expectancy
    and confidence.
only God can make this miracle happen ...
    it could come tomorrow and i could be there
    and see it.

november 18

virginia, minnesota. a gray, cold, bleak day.
    bev wenshau's here with me.
today is our twenty-mile run.
even bev (with five marathons under her belt) says
    that on days like this she gets scared.
    can she survive it?

we're wondering where we're going to run and
what the surface is going to be like.

she and i talked last night about faithfulness . . .
about being true.
about making a commitment and following through.
i'm so glad for bev today . . . the chance to run with her
and get prepared for israel.
not only is running the most disciplined thing
i've ever done . . .
going to israel is the greatest test of faith . . .
the scariest thing i've encountered.
running is so measurable . . . that's what humbles me.
often the measurable results are not what i want
them to be.

soo . . . i get up, pull on tights, shorts, sweat shirt.
pull my hair back in a ponytail.
i trust His power and not my own . . . His strength.
i move out knowing that again today
He will be faithful.
Jesus is in me . . . warm, vibrant, alive . . . this day.

november 20

thinking again about marty . . . the student in oregon.

that reminded me of the evening i had dinner with
a good friend in the suburbs of boston.
she's a Christian v.i.p.—a great mind and heart
in a world of mediocre thoughts and
shallow commitments.

116   tasty chicken. (i love home cooking. food must be one of God's best ideas.)

before a warm, comfortable fire, she suddenly looked at me and said,

"ann, when are you going to stop reporting to the world how great 'ann' is, and start telling them how good God is?"

i was unable to speak. devastated. fought tears.
no one ever had said that to me before.
    it had never entered my mind ...
i tried to be open ... to say "yes" to honest criticism.
stammered some weak, trite statements in response.
    riding back into boston on the train ...
my tears screamed out my embarrassment and pain.
and the horror that if what my friend said is true,
    then my whole life has been wasted.

"oh, Jesus, no. please.
it isn't true.
Jesus, i know i am human ... i have an ego.
i fail.
but Jesus, bring into my life whatever i need
to be centered ... pure ... honest.
to make Your song live, and not my own.
forgive me, Lord.
forgive me."

december 19

it's the day before my first marathon.
   tiberius ... israel.
i have never been so scared. i feel really weak and
   inadequate ... inexperienced.
   i'm afraid of failure ...
of knowing the whole world is saying,

   "ann, we knew you were crazy
   six months ago, when you started
   this thing."

the hotel doesn't know anything about spaghetti
   or fettucini ... (the runner's favorite source of
   stable carbohydrate).
there has been no time to adjust to the time change ...
   or the ten-hour flight.
two young israelis took bev and me along the
   marathon route. i ate twenty chocolate-chip cookies
   my friend donna had made for me.
the driver kept staring at me in the rear-view mirrow.
   i watched him. he told me later he was shocked
   that i kept popping all those cookies into my mouth.
   he was worried that i would get sick.

all day, i have hardly even breathed. a strange land.
   far from home. all the children won't arrive
   until midnight.

i insisted that cindy smith (who is going to meet us
   on the fifteenth mile and run the last eleven
   with us) and bev and i all stay together that night.
   we finally turned out the lights.

i lay rigid, in tears, all through the
        long night hours.
        i wanted to sleep ... knew i needed to ... but
        couldn't stop the pounding of my heart.

in one bed ... cindy, sleeping soundly.
        cindy, the athlete. the ex-track coach.
        one marathon under her belt.
in the other bed ... bev, snoring lightly.
        five marathons on her record.
        no big deal.

i felt small ... lost ... fragile.
when the sun brought light to my piece of the world,
        in this little hotel room on the sea of galilee,
        i was so relieved.

faithfulness means you never just walk away.
        you face your mountain.
you shake your fist at the attempts of satan,
        or anyone else, who tries to drag you down.

i have paid my dues. done my homework.
        run all the miles.
        faithful with my end of the bargain.
now God will fulfill His part.
        i haven't seen Him do it yet ... and it seems
a pretty big undertaking ... even for God ...
        but i have to believe He will.

and this i know about faithfulness ...

        God is trustworthy.

119   in october, when i began to feel God wanted me
            to take some children with me to israel,
        i began to pray that Jesus would show me which
            children in boston should go.
        joseph . . . tracy . . . charlie . . . pablo . . . alison . . .
            i began to choose them.
        black, puerto rican, spanish, jewish, caucasian.

        pablo's parents do not speak english.
            i had to take an interpreter.
            his father's eyes moistened.

            "you mean i have spent my whole life
            saving money to bring my family to america,
            and you want to take my young pablo to
            israel for Christmas?"

        to him, it was incredible.

        i finally chose twelve children to go with me.
            nine adults to help.
        they all have red teeshirts to wear the day of the
            marathon . . . the shirts say, in big white letters:

            "WE'RE ANN'S KIDS."
        my very own cheering squad. yahoo!

december 20

        tiberius. *the* day.
            my first marathon. what all my training has been for.

cindy raced in with toast and honey at 5:30 a.m.
bev and i coated our toes with vaseline.
added bandaids where a blister even *might* appear.
pinned the numbers on our teeshirts.

what if i did not run fast enough to qualify
for boston...
three hours, twenty minutes?
everyone said it had never been done by someone who
had been running only about six months.
but neither can anyone imagine that i'd have another
chance to run a marathon between this one and
the boston in april. most runners don't run more
than one marathon a year... or two at the most,
spaced far apart.

runners were moving in little circles... lying on the
ground... stretching... leaning against trees
and pulling their achilles tendons.
they all looked young and strong and lean and like
veterans.
bev and i spotted only a few women.

for a moment i actually felt the earth would open
and swallow me. that this was a nightmare...
a wild and fanciful dream.
i could not even remember what it felt like to run
one mile... i could not imagine 26.2 miles.

a man walked up to me... obviously a participant
in the race.

"where are you from?"

"the united states. and you?"

"canada ... toronto ... uh, may i ask your name?"

"sure. it's ann kiemel."

"ann! i thought you might be. my wife and i have read all your books."

the children all had their teeshirts on. they were
   wide-eyed. lively. enthusiastic.
people began to watch all those children ... and me.
   curious about the teeshirts declaring,
   "we're ann's kids."
from the stares, i guessed that many thought i was
   too young for such a large family. smile.

the israeli cameramen were all ready.
   it has been decided that the marathon should be
   part of the documentary.
   talk about pressure!
just before the starting gun went off, the israeli
   national television cameramen, who had come to
   film the german expected to win, changed their
   minds and decided to build their focus and
   presentation around me.

the gun popped. with tears in my eyes, i squeezed
   bev's hand, and we started into this most
   unbelievable experience of my life.
   my greatest test.
   the tallest mountain.

a couple of young runners kept pushing into
        bev and me.
        they saw the cameras zeroing in and they wanted
        to be seen.

        "please, sir, move over. you are crowding me,"
        i'd say.

        "uh, sir . . . we can't breathe. please give us room,"
        bev would help me.

that went on all through the first sixteen miles,
        as they did their best to be televised.

gady, the head cameraman for the documentary,
        was ahead of me most of the way in a moving car.
a deep warmth kept springing up in me for this
        new friend.
        i'd call out now and then . . .

        "gady, i'm doing it.
        gady, hi!"

only the top of his head showed over the camera.

at the fifth mile my face was flushed . . .
        and my pain began. right at the beginning of the run.
        my body was too tense . . . tight . . . it was too warm.
        we kept squeezing wet sponges on our arms and
        necks to keep cooled down.

i began to beg for coke . . . something ice cold, with
        some energy in it.
        in my heart, i kept beseeching . . .

"God, give me this mountain . . .
        i'll run straight to the finish."

i figured i could suffer anything for another
    hour and a half.
    another 45 minutes . . .
    another 30 minutes.
at mile 20, israeli television pulled up beside us . . .
    (cindy had joined us at the fifteenth mile,
    just as i had done for her in the new york marathon).

    "ann, we hear you like to sing little songs.
    sing us one now. . . ."

and they stuck a microphone on a long pole out the
    window and into my face.

by this time, i was in so much pain i could
    barely talk.
    if cindy bumped into me on one side, i'd snap . . .
    "move over!"

nothing comforted me . . . not the sea of galilee . . .
    or thinking about Jesus living there . . .
    or my dream for Him . . .
nothing could be a help except getting to the finish line.
however, bev and cindy helped me sing, and then i
    tagged one more song on at the end.

omri or herb fisher would stick a can of coke
    (a dollar a can in israel)
into my hand as i passed certain mile points.
every time i gulped down a few swallows . . . it only

meant i had to go on with this nightmare.
        there were miles and miles to go.
    people were waiting at the finish . . . and thousands
        more were listening all over the united states.

    about mile 23, i jerked to a stop, and said,

        "cindy, you and bev go on.
        i'm going to walk a little."

        "*no,* you are *not!*" screamed cindy.

        "yes, i am. i mean it. i have to. . . ."

    cindy grabbed my teeshirt and began literally to
        drag me along for about twenty yards.
    my legs eventually stopped fighting the pull, and
        fell back into rhythm.
    the whole thing seemed absolutely eternal.

    back at the start of the race, when national television
        had pushed in among the runners and with
        microphone in hand, asked me why i was running
        and how i felt . . .
    bev said right then and there she decided to run
        at my side, whatever my pace . . .
        and stay with me the whole way.
    she said she had never seen me cry, but kept
        noticing tears in my eyes.
        kept feeling the pressure i must have been under
        with two sets of television cameras on me,
        and the world, in a sense, watching.

125   for me this was one of the most powerful, purest
expressions of love i have ever known.
never had i so needed a faithful friend at my side.
never was i so scared about running alone.
i feel confident that bev could have
qualified herself for the boston marathon . . .
could really have shone . . .
she relinquished it all . . . to stay with me.

no one can ever take that away from me.
i will never forget the magnitude of that love.

suddenly i looked ahead and could see . . . faintly . . .
the little flags that lined the final two-tenths of a mile.
then i realized we were turning down the final
stretch.

i began to quote scripture . . . panting it out . . .
gasping for air between words . . .

"bless the Lord . . . oh, my soul . . .
and all . . . that is within . . . me . . .
bless His . . . holy name.
bless the Lord . . . oh, my soul . . .
and forget not all . . . His benefits. . . ."

my legs picked up the pace a little. i reached out
and grabbed bev's hand. she squeezed mine,
and we came bounding across the finish line. . . .
tears spilling from our hollow, dark eyes.
our bodies suddenly came to a stop.
children and adults pulled my teeshirt and
kissed even my grimy arms . . .
hugged my head.

our time: three hours, thirty-five minutes.
not a qualifying time, but a very good time for
   marathon number one.

the microphone in my face again.
   "ann, when is your next marathon?"

   "i don't know. i can't bear to think of another
   one right now."

   "why did you do it?"

   "because i follow Jesus.
   He plants dreams in my heart.
   i did it to prove that God is great,
   and any dream He gives can live."

the next day, we all watched the television presentation.
it was a shock to see myself coming across the finish line,
   looking so fresh. so vital.
   as if i had just stepped out of a sauna.
   relaxed . . . voice steady . . . radiant.

my mountain had been faced . . . the battle tackled.
   the fear of the unknown was gone . . .
   because it was no longer an unknown.
i had finished the race . . . and had won—
(no, i didn't qualify.
no, i wasn't by any means the first one to finish.
but . . . i had prepared.
i had been faithful every single day beforehand.)
   i had prayed,

"God, whatever it means,
just throw me into the battle
and let me get it behind me."

i could sleep without nightmares. i could pour
myself into the rest of our time in israel
because i had done what i came to do.

and in bedouin camps for miles...
in barracks and soldiers' tents all across that
amazing little country...
over bar tables and above kitchen sinks in kibbutzes,
people had heard me speak the name of Jesus
and had watched me run the race.
and His name... His will... gives power.

my israeli film crew says,

"ann, in israel, you are famous. everyone watched
you run the marathon. and ann, something
happened to us while we filmed you. your eyes
reflected so much determination that we felt
we lived inside your soul,
running with you.
though we had six hours of work that day, to
us it seemed like twenty minutes.
we were so stirred... wanting you to make it.
to us, it was a miracle."

to me, it was a miracle, too...
alleluia, alleluia... amen.

what is faith? it is the confident assurance that something we want is going to happen.
hebrews 11:1

december 24

Christmas eve in bethlehem. shepherds' field.
  carols sung in faraway corners.
  under timeless skies.
we touched the rocks and trees and waters that
  once were touched by Jesus, our Lord.
our eyes searched for miles, through bus windows,
  to catch the flavor of His love in vast,
  rocky wilderness.
  our voices were silent.
then simple children's songs burst from the depths
  of our hearts.
  we will never be the same.

the last night, pablo wanted to see me "privately."
i led him down the hotel corridor, to a quiet spot.
  he threw his arms around me,
  his small body shaking with sobs.
  in broken english he said,

  "oh, ann, you have changed my whole life.
  my whole world."

  "my dear little pablo, you have changed mine.
  you are a chosen child who will someday
  brave impossible challenges,
  and with God in your heart,
  you will change the world."

faithfulness is listening for the call.
  waiting for the dream.
knowing there are dozens of dreams to be born
  in us.

knowing they come only as we say *"yes"* to them.
as we open our lives wide to the living,
conquering Christ...
and give Him a home within our lives.

faithfulness means God can trust us with great ideas
and magnificent adventures.
with young children whose searching eyes watch
for values and causes worth dying for.
children who will someday be giants in God's plan
for the world.

january 7

christmas is past... i'm back from israel, rome...
from san francisco with my family at new years....
a t.v. appearance in canada.
back home.
now the boston marathon is staring me in the face...
and i'm not qualified.
what am i to do?

yesterday, while running, i kept asking Jesus:

"i'll do anything, Jesus, but please show me.
unless i know it's from You, i don't think i could
possibly go back into training so soon... to pour
myself into all the long miles, knowing i very easily
might not qualify for boston. but if You are calling
me, i can face anything."

i felt assured that the Lord would love me either way.
	that it was my choice. He is with me, regardless.
	again, there are no guarantees.
	that's the way it is with faithfulness.

as i was thinking over these things, i suddenly
	remembered something that happened to me about
	two months before Christmas. while i was training
	for israel.
one day steve and i boarded a delta flight going to
	atlanta. it was the middle of a twenty-one-day
	trip . . . i was worn out and didn't want to be close
	to anyone.
choosing the first seat, i strapped my little bag into
	the empty seat next to me, and leaned my head
	back to rest.

a man stopped and started to crawl over me, to sit
	in that empty seat. he was a pilot . . .
	i could tell by his uniform.
looking into his face, i scowled as forbiddingly as
	i could. the last thing i wanted was someone sitting
	next to me . . . someone i would feel responsible for.
he actually drew back for a moment. (he said later
	the look almost finished him.)
then his mouth set in a very determined way . . .
he coldly stepped across and asked me to
	remove my bag.
	i did.

soon i began to feel very bad about my attitude.
i travel all over the world, speaking about God's love . . .

then this. what a way to act. awful.
reaching over, i tapped him on the shoulder.

"sir, please forgive me.
i don't usually act like this.
i've been traveling a long time . . . i'm tired.
i just didn't want to be close to anyone.
sir, i'm a christian . . . and i know i am supposed
to be more positive . . . but one of the reasons i love
Jesus so much is that He understands me on days
like this."

charlie (later i learned his name) threw his head
back and laughed.

"oh, i understand. i feel very much like you
do today."

we had been airborne awhile, and i noticed that
charlie was looking through a *runners' world*
magazine. nudging him, i asked . . .

"are you a runner?"

"yeah, i've been one for years . . . but now i'm
thinking of doing a marathon. i've always wanted
to . . . and there is a good one in new orleans in
february that i'm going for."

it was an incredible trip. i had a beautiful chance to
share with charlie my faith in Jesus Christ.
and i never forgot his mentioning that new orleans
26.2-mile race.

maybe that's the one i should enter ... maybe there i
would qualify for boston.

january 8

investigated the new orleans marathon. it will be on
february 10 ... but the deadline for applications
was december 31. too late.

however, i wrote a letter to the race director explaining
that i had been out of the country ... had run
israel ... and hoped they would accept me because
i very much desire to qualify for boston. that it is
winter now, and there were not many marathons
available, especially somewhere with the probability
of decent weather.

january 12

without ever having really stopped, i went back
into training for new orleans ... a race only six weeks
after israel.

the weather has turned unbelievably cold in boston.

often i get up and run in weather 20 degrees below zero.
come back with my eyelashes frozen with ice
and eyes red and watering.

back to ten miles a day ... one twenty-mile run a week.

back to getting into a cab at my building, and asking the
cabbie to drive me twenty miles out and drop me
off ... to run back in.

even though the cab drivers make $26 for that trip,
they become so traumatized by the twentieth
mile that they try to talk me out of it.

"lady, i can't just let you off here.
you'll never make it all the way back in."

"oh, yes, sir . . . don't worry. i can."

"but, lady, it's raining" or
"it's so cold and windy . . ." or
"but you're so far away from everything."

and i respond,

"i know; i don't want to, but i *must*.
it's hard work, but that's part of a dream.
you've got to be tough."

and i crawl out of the cab with tears in my eyes,
and start running toward home. . . .
a dollar bill (which i've never had to use)
in one shoe. i don't stop until i see
lewis wharf and the lobby door . . .
not for water . . .
not for anything.

january 15

received letters from two members of the israeli
film crew . . .
heartwarming.

dear ann:

*i feel like writing to you. i hope there are less mistakes with
my english than to talk to you.*

*i'm working in the film business about seventeen years
and honestly i have to tell you this is the first time in a
project that i'm involved, besides taking care of the sound,
with emotion.*

*We are in different religion, but there is nothing
to do with this. i really appreciate in what
you believe and i enjoy when i hear you speaking to people,
and when you stopped us a few times during the
shooting and prayed (which is unusual for us).
it was really great.*

*remember when we had the party with the kids and
you asked me to say one word only. i said "power"
because i feel you have the power to influence
people to believe, and it's great.*

*yours, love,
eli*

dearest ann,

*shalom, shalom! i was deeply touched to receive
your letter and must confess not the least taken
aback by its warmth. throughout our time together
i felt the presence of a warm guiding hand.*

*my deep-felt thanks for the warmth you radiated
during our filming and for the strong belief
you gave and planted in us. suddenly it dawned on me
that those things that are done in a spirit of
goodwill and with love are truly* good.

*it's sad to remember that so many things have to
be done in our little world, but from you i received the courage and strength to walk against
the darkness, through the cold winds that bar
our paths, and to have crystallized by your in-
spiration my desire to light the way for all the
sad and lonely people.*

*i believe He really cares for us and will enable us
to meet again, and to follow and achieve our goals.*

hoping to see you soon . . .
gady

this is my day for letters. major general arter,
of fort lesley j. mcnair in washington, d.c.
wrote this . . .

dear ann,

happy new year!

*easily, i have written, mentally, about 1000 times
to tell you how very much i enjoyed sharing time
with you this past july 4. in each of those
letters, i've thanked you for the nice words that
you included in your book. super book.*

*this morning, paul miller announced in our
weekly staff meeting of your splendid israel
marathon run. congratulations. you have pro-
jected yet another inspirational act.*

*when you next travel to the washington area, i ask,
if at all possible, that you please share with us
as much time as your schedule permits. meanwhile,
i send my very best.*

sincerely. . . .

after i talked with major general arter last july,
  he started making his men run two miles a day!
i wonder how they liked that . . . smile.

january 17

a letter finally came from new orleans.

"no, we're sorry, but the deadline is past.
we cannot accept you as an entrant."

i took the letter to jock. my heart felt calm and
  steady. somehow, i just know new orleans
  is my race. God will work it out.
by chance i had run into charlie lowry, the delta pilot.
  he had developed a bad knee injury
  and wasn't planning to run the whole marathon . . .
  but he said he would love to meet me there
  and pace me the first ten miles to
  get me started.

jock sat right down and wrote a letter to
george de dual, the director of the new orleans race.
will his letter make the difference?

january 26

it's a clear day . . . with forty-mile-an-hour gale winds.
i'm due for a twenty-mile run.
i'll have to run it alone today . . . can't find anyone
to do it with me.
i'm sitting here feeling that gnawing fear again . . .
that overwhelming sense of responsibility.
to give my best . . . be disciplined . . . keep my life
in order.
i know that when i finish the twenty miles i'll feel
like a new person and life will hold a different
perspective for me.
i have to hang on to "no gain without pain" . . . to
realize that i have to give my best.

the other day a man called long distance. i don't
even know him, but he said, "did you win?"
"well, sir," i answered. "let me tell you about
marathons . . . no one wins, unless you're world class
and the first one over the line. but if you mean, was i
faithful in all my practice runs and my training,
and did i give it my best and did i finish? then,
yes, i won . . . i really won."

another person wrote and said, "it's great you did
a marathon. my son and i did a six-mile

marathon recently." smile.
i find that most people don't know that a
marathon is twenty-six, point two miles... and most
of the world doesn't understand what it really
takes to run that kind of distance.

i'm thankful today that my body is strong
and healthy.
no aches or pains.
thankful today that i have Jesus.
i really want Him to be glorified.
i really do surrender this to Him.

so i guess i'd better get my shorts on...
my knee socks... my running shoes...
and head on out.

january 29

spent all day at the superior court with tony.
i'll tell you this... the court system puts the
fear of the law into you.
it inspires you to obedience as you watch people
walk in and out of the courtrooms with
red eyes and tears...
penalties having to be faced.

went to jenny and louis's for dinner last night.
played checkers with stancey,
scrabble with joseph and jenny.
took the children caramel apples... held the baby.

140   came back and worked in my office until eleven.
       a hard, tiring day . . . but a good one.
       because Jesus is Lord and i was able to move through
         His world in His presence and His Spirit . . .
         and represent Him.

february 1

ten-mile run in concord, mass. late afternoon . . .
  very cold—in the teens . . . getting dark.
cindy smith is visiting me and she ran the miles
  with me.
up the last hill and down the final stretch, in the
  blue-dark, cold, quiet town, our voices rang out as
  we sang, triumphantly . . .

  for the joy set before Him . . .
  for the joy He endured the pain . . .
  for the joy He suffered the shame . . .
  and He'd do it all again. . . .

                                    —ray hildebrand

faithfulness is measurable . . . observable.
  either i ran my miles today . . . or i did not.
  either three miles . . . or ten.
  forty minutes . . . or an hour.
  i ate dessert . . . or stayed on my diet.
  i got up when the alarm went off . . . or i stayed
  in bed longer.
  i finished the term project . . .
  or arrived at the meeting on time . . .

or washed the dishes ... or i didn't.
i was honest ... or i was dishonest.

it brings a sense of reality to our lives.
    no games ... no lies ... no cheating.
faithfulness puts it on the line.

when i was young, it seemed to me that if one was
    good in math, if one was brilliant,
    one would be utterly respected
    and greatly loved.
if i could only sing well, or play the piano,
    or make everyone believe i was skilled in tennis ...
    i would be far more valuable.

today, i know the reality: that i will never be good in
    math or brilliant at the piano.
    for me that is not real.
one cannot be faithful to anything that is not real.
    not ever.

following Jesus is measurable too.
    either i desire Him with my whole heart ...
    soul, mind, strength ... or i don't.

often, in athletics, the secret is the coach.
children will swim or run through long work-outs
    and with great pain ...
just because they love and respect their coaches.
some have cried through training periods,
    but come back day after day because of
    fierce loyalty to their leader.

142   if we could just fall in love with Jesus.
if only we could love Him so much that
    every day we would be unwilling to
    give less than our best . . .
that our eyes would sparkle and shine.
our hands would always be open and warm
    and ready to touch a shoulder . . .
    or pat a child . . . or rake someone's yard.
our laughter would be free and frequent.
our energy and zest would be magnetic and
    soothing and easy-flowing.
the whole world would know our Coach.
would take notice of the race . . . and watch.

we would command respect for Him.

the fresh sunrise and clear morning air
    would carry to all the dark corners
    that a Leader lives . . .
    and He sets all men free.

february 7

the new orleans marathon is next sunday . . .
    still no word about my application
    since jock wrote his letter.
jock has been urging me to find another marathon.

    "shoot, ye don't want to go clear
    to new orleans anyways. . . ."

we know how dearly God loves us, and we feel this warm love everywhere within us because God has given us the Holy Spirit to fill our hearts with His love. romans 5:5

"jock, i feel it in my heart.
            that's my race."

today i came in from my ten-mile morning run
            and knelt by my bed.
            never have i been more sincere . . .

            "Jesus, i give You this marathon.
            i give You my running.
            whether i am supposed to qualify or not.
            go . . . stay . . .
            only one thing really matters . . . Your will.
            please have Your will."

this afternoon i went over to jock's office
            at the boston garden.
was going to pick up an application for some other
            marathon he had discovered.
            had relinquished new orleans, if necessary.

            "jock, i'm here to pick up that form."

            "oh . . . yeah, yeah . . ."

there was something in his eyes, though.

            "jock, you didn't hear from new orleans today,
            did you?"

a slight smile . . . a twinkle in his eye.

            "jock, *did you?*" i screamed.

145　　　"yeah, i did ... it took those goons long enough
　　　　to let us know."

he was excited too ... almost as if he really believed
　　Jesus was in it. he showed me the letter.

dear mr. semple:

*thank you for your communication dated january 17,
1980. i can well appreciate the dilemma your young
friend faces, as i have, on occasion, experienced
the same problem. she appears to be quite an amazing
person and i look forward to seeing her.*

*if you will be so kind as to have her fill
out the enclosed application and have it
returned to me immediately, i will be
happy to waive the time period in question.*

*yours very truly,
george b. de dual*

february 8

my plane reservations had been made a long time ago,
　　on faith.
some of my dearest friends, rolfe and dot mccollister,
　　from baton rouge, were expecting me and waiting.
　　cindy smith agreed to let me bring her along ...
　　to meet me at the fifteenth mile and finish
　　the race with me again.

we both decided to wear exactly what we had worn
in our other marathons. white terrycloth shorts and
red adidas teeshirts that once belonged to sally berry.
the mccollisters own two apartments in the french
quarter of new orleans. that is where we will stay.
dot has a women's retreat, so rolfe and stephen,
their college-age son, drove cindy and me over
there tonight.
rolfe fed us lots of cookies and spaghetti
and doughnuts.

february 9

a very gray saturday. went to pick up my number
(#240) and charlie's.
we drove along the full route of the race. i felt
a cloud coming over my heart . . . tension in my
hands. they kept fidgeting in my lap.

most of the race would take place on a
twenty-two-mile bridge . . . the longest in the world.
an all cement and steel structure.
flat except for two big rises, under which ships pass.
one bulge at the eighth mile . . .
another bulge at the eighteenth.
plus two miles at the beginning and the end
of the bridge.
when one is riding in a car for twenty-six miles,
it seems like an eternal distance.
tyndale house publishers had hired a photographer to
cover the race . . . he was in the back seat with me.

everyone was talking ... except me. i wanted to crawl
  under the seat and hide ... not watch all the
  long miles ... see those bulges in the road.
  this was my showdown ... this was it ...
  my very last chance to make it to the
  boston maraton.
if Jesus helps me, though, i know i can.
  and there's no turning back. period.

this evening we picked charlie up from his flight.
i hardly knew him except for that airplane encounter.
before we all headed for our various rooms for the
  night, we stretched and got our clothes
  laid out ... and picked up some giant
  oatmeal cookies.
rolfe got the Bible out and talked with us
  and we each prayed. even charlie.
i don't think he had ever prayed aloud before,
  but it was powerful.

  "God, even though i'm usually a strong runner,
  and now am injured ...
  and though i can't run the whole marathon
  tomorrow, i think this is the most exciting
  and significant race i've ever done."

february 10

at five a.m. the alarm went off. i had slept soundly.
  the room was dark, cold.
cindy and i lay there in our beds, feeling the

the sun lives in the heavens where God placed
it and moves out across the skies...as joyous
as an athlete looking forward to a race!
psalm 19:4, 5

149   tremendous test ... the challenge of that day.
        she prayed ... then i did.
     out we jumped ... she fixed toast for all of us,
        and we stretched and dressed and "greased up."
     everything was in order ... even the weather.
        32°. (i do my best in semi-cold weather.)
     the race was to start at eight a.m.

     rolfe and stephen and cindy dropped charlie and me
        at the starting point, and went on to take
        cindy to the fifteenth-mile point on the bridge.
        the wind was howling. we felt chilled, but knew
        our bodies would soon heat up in the race.
     i was dressed in knee socks, shorts, and teeshirt,
        with long socks on my arms for warmth ...
        knowing i could pull them off and drop them
        when the chill wore off.
     charlie got us places close to the front with the
        world class runners, so we wouldn't lose time
        moving out.
     a young man on my left tapped me and smiled,
        "good luck!"
        i hugged him. "you too!"

     again i found tears in my eyes. so much was at stake.
        i was ready ... but i was scared.
     charlie squeezed my hand ... the gun went off.
     though charlie and i had never run together before,
        he was a pro ... my friend.

     i ran, knowing i would run as hard and as fast
        as i could
        to the very end, no matter how much it hurt.

i wouldn't stop until the finish line . . . (unless i
dropped dead somewhere along the route.)
that was settled.

patti lyons, from boston, a world class runner, was
there on the press bus. she screamed for me
as they passed.
at the fifteenth mile i could see cindy, wind blowing
her hair . . . jumping up and down . . . waving her
hands in the air.
she was smiling . . . her fist raised in a victory sign.

"c'mon, ann. yahoo! you're right on schedule.
you can do it."

then she was running with me . . . but i was getting
very tired. i gasped, "cindy, sing . . ."
or "cindy, pray . . ." or "oh, cindy, i'm dying!"
the last water station was mile twenty-two.
at that point i was in more acute physical pain than
i had ever experienced in a lifetime.
four and a half miles of that kind of pain seemed
not only intimidating, but absolutely impossible
to survive. my mind began to play tricks on me.
i felt claustrophobic . . . closed in, as if i was
actually smothering.
in my mind i kept picturing one thing . . . the finish line.
the jubilance . . . the smiles . . . the celebration.
if i could get there fast enough . . . if i could just
keep going.

a mile off the bridge, with one more to go, i gasped,

"cindy . . . cindy . . . i can't!"

"you can!" she screamed.

i knew i could ... i knew i would ... nothing could have
   made me stop. i just wanted to hear her say it! ...
   to know she was there.

my sense of reality was gone. i couldn't even see
   all the bystanders, cheering. i just heard them
   vaguely, as from a great distance.
in those eleven miles with cindy, she had not told
   me whether my time was good or bad, and
   i was too terrified to ask.
in the last half mile i no longer cared ... not for
   food or drink or to qualify ... hardly even to live.
i only wanted to see the finish line so i could stop
   and know i had given it my best ...
   and stop suffering.

"ann, ann, it's right around the corner."

"where ... where?" and my voice drifted away.

it took every thread of inner reserve ... of physical
   and mental strength ... to push on to the finish.

(my friend raymond berry had told me, "ann, you've
   done your miles. stored them in the bank.
   february 10, all you have to do is draw them out."
during the whole race, i thought of that. i know
   that day i drew out every single mile and every drop
   of sweat and ounce of courage i had put in!)

the finish line was in sight. suddenly i could see
   the streamers.

just as i crossed the line, i looked up at the clock.

3:18. i had done it. could it really be?

"oh, Jesus, thank You . . . cindy, cindy, where are
you? cindy, we did it!"

tears . . . people i didn't know, holding me up. a second
   when i thought i would be sick at my stomach . . .
   but wasn't. rolfe and stephen crying too.
someone led me to a grassy spot. cindy helped me
   stretch to keep from tightening up.
blistered feet . . . big, ugly blisters.
throbbing ankles . . . a thousand balloons . . . garbage
   cans painted yellow . . . the sky one great sunrise.
i couldn't stop crying . . . and laughing. but my heart
   was calm and quiet. streams in dry places.
   floods on barren ground.
the banner was out there for everyone to see, waving
   proudly.

"oh, Jesus . . . oh, Jesus . . .
faithful . . . faithful Lord.
You did this great thing in me . . .
and i'll never forget."

it was the greatest moment in my life . . . bar none.
a moment when i knew more deeply than ever before
   that Jesus is . . . that He is love . . .
   that love is good . . . that love never fails . . .
   "great is Thy faithfulness, Lord, unto me."

charlie had dropped back from cindy and me at the
   twentieth mile . . . but he did finish the marathon . . .

his first . . . in 3:44.

there's something about running a marathon together . . .
    sharing a common dream.

knowing the price the other has paid . . . because you
    have paid a price too.

hurting . . . thinking nothing could be so bad . . .
    but still not quitting.
    finishing . . . knowing the victory that comes . . .
    not cheaply, but with a very high price.

charlie will be my friend for life. no one can take
    from me that moment we shared. it is a part of the
    fiber of who i am today.

i think charlie is really going to know God, too.
    someday.

we ran that bridge together . . . felt the wind and cold
    air . . . and pain . . . together.
    and felt God's love covering it all.

february 28

one of the israeli film crew that covered
    my documentary called my hotel room
    in los angeles . . .

"ann, tonight i had dinner with a group of my
friends from israel who are here working for
paramount studios. they wanted to know all about
this project i am on. who is this 'ann kiemel'? what
makes her so religious? to so deeply believe in Jesus?

"ann, i got very excited trying to tell them.
about your courage in the marathon.
your neighborhood.
the little gymnasium.

"suddenly, i felt this tear running down the
side of my face. i was so embarrassed.
i did not know what to do.
everyone in the whole restaurant, i thought,
was watching this tear on my face.

"i reached up and quietly wiped the tear away...
when an amazing thing happened. a second
tear followed it. when i wiped it away,
a third one came.
ann ... i was trying to tell them about your faith ...
and the tears kept coming, and i did not
know what to do."

march 3

jeff wells came to los angeles to be a part of a
    tape project with me.
he is in training for the summer olympics in moscow.
    we ran fifteen and a half miles, away from the
    hotel ... and back.
i sang him little songs ...
    he quoted scripture to me.
then we ate all the homemade peanut butter cookies
    his girlfriend had sent with him.

march 7

flew all night with jan and baby nash (three months
old) from san francisco to cleveland. jan has been
helping me with the taping too. tom kept tre at home.

jan became very ill in the cleveland airport . . .
5:30 a.m. . . . before tom arrived to pick her up . . .
so i scooped up tiny nash . . . caught a 6:10 a.m.
connection, and brought him home with me.
i am exhausted . . . desk covered with stacks of
unanswered mail . . . phone messages not
yet returned.

march 8

took baby nash to the berry's so i could run my
twenty-one miles.
joanne ferguson picked me up and clocked the miles.
i can't count the times she's stood with me like that.
35° . . . pouring rain . . . much colder than i thought.
tried to pump my arms to generate more energy inside.
socks and two sweat shirts and shoes absolutely soaked.
at least five extra pounds.

hard run. emotional. rain beat against my face
and threatened to ruin my good nature!
mud puddles everywhere.
celebrated the finish.

berrys brought dinner . . . and the baby . . . in.
what great people!

11 p.m. . . . little nash and i flew to cleveland so i could return him to his parents and pick up my connection in the morning for columbia, south carolina, where i speak tomorrow.

march 9

south carolina . . . warm, lovely people.
   steve is back . . . now married . . . still my road
   manager. still like my brother.

after i spoke, two university students ran almost
   six miles with me in the dark . . . ten p.m.

march 11

for many years, i have said,

   "life is not made up of big moments . . . but
   ordinary days, when there is no one to pat you on
   the back or cheer you, or notice. you must give your
   best on ordinary days, and big moments will come
   only now and then."

i have said this because my mother said it first.
   all my growing-up years.

it is true.
two great marathons are over. behind me.
   i have qualified for boston and am in the

peak of training for it.
i'm in the ordinary days... the nitty-gritty.
the grueling... the often mundane and difficult.
where most of life takes place.
a shin splint on one leg.
a swollen, sore achilles tendon on the other.

a twenty-one-mile run is scheduled for tomorrow...
i will be in calgary, alberta, so must run in
totally unknown territory... after seven hours
of flying and a three-hour time change.
before i speak.

i've been rereading a letter i got from pablo...
if anything will help me get ready for boston
it will be the love of friends like little pablo:

dear ann,

i feel lonely. me without you, bev, steve,
joanne is nothing. the day when the boston
marathon comes i going to wear my teeshirt
of you, ann, and i going to run with you
three miles. you are getting ready to win
that marathon with Jesus again. you did it
last time with Jesus, and you will do it and do it.
i really miss you.

pablo

yes, pablo.

i "press toward the mark."
with one song to sing... His song.

the faithful Savior's song.
i hear my Drummer.
i feel His pace.
i will not turn back.

only a few win the prize...

i'm running to win.

epilogue

yes, i ran the boston marathon. number W327.
i was scared...
a scorching hot day...
one and a half million witnesses
along the way.
my town... my turf... my people.

i made one bad mistake.
because it was so hot
i discarded my heavy knee socks
for some light, cool foot socks.
not enough protection against blisters.
it cost me...
proved my novice status!

tears filled my eyes as my blistered feet
hit the pavement over... and over...
and over.

when i am afraid, i will put my confidence in
You. yes, i will trust the promises of God.
psalm 56:3, 4

then someone would reach out a hand
      and steady me . . .
      put a cup of liquid in my hand . . .
      wave a sign with my name on it . . .
      and Jesus' name.
   friends along the way would cheer me on . . .
      scream out the titles of my books . . .
      anything to keep me going . . .
      to help me not to quit.

   then i saw the finish line.
      i gasped and pushed on . . .
      and smiled as i thought of Jesus . . .
      and of jock and tom and jan.
      of dr. taylor and joanne and raymond berry.
      and all my children from israel.

   i was running to the finish . . . for them.

   as i crossed the line, i knew i had passed
      the final test
      of a long year's dream. alleluia. amen.